Soul Retreats™

Presented To: Elaine Teague

Presented By: Faye Robbins

Date: May 2003

Soul Retreats™ for Women
ISBN 0-310-98902-7

Copyright 2002 by GRQ Ink, Inc.
1948 Green Hills Boulevard
Franklin, Tennessee 37067

"Soul Retreats" is a trademark owned by GRQ, Inc.

Published by Inspirio™, The gift group of Zondervan
5300 Patterson Avenue, SE
Grand Rapids, Michigan 49530

All Scripture quotations, unless otherwise noted, are taken from the *Holy Bible: New International Version* (North American Edition) ®. Copyright 1973, 1978, 1984, by International Bible Society. Used by permission of Zondervan. All rights reserved.

The "NIV" and "New International Version" trademarks are registered in the United States Patent and Trademark Office by International Bible Society.

Scripture quotations noted GNT are taken from GOOD NEWS TRANSLATION, SECOND EDITION, Copyright © 1992 by American Bible Society. Used by permission. All rights reserved.

Scripture quotations noted NASB are taken from the NEW AMERICAN STANDARD BIBLE ®, Copyright © 1960, 1962, 1963, 1968, 1971, 1973, 1975, 1977, 1995 by the Lockman Foundation. Used by permission.

Scripture quotations noted NRSV are taken from the New Revised Standard Version of the bible, copyright 1989 by the Division of Christian Education of the National Council of the Churches of Christ in the USA. Used by permission. All rights reserved.

Scripture quotations noted KJV are from the King James Version of the Bible.

All rights reserved. No part of this publication may be reproduced, stored in a retrieval system, or transmitted in any form or by any means—electronic, mechanical, photocopy, recording, or any other—except for brief quotations in printed reviews, without the prior permission of the publisher.

Requests for information should be addressed to:
Inspirio™, The gift group of Zondervan
Grand Rapids, Michigan 49530

http://www.inspiriogifts.com

Editor and Compiler: Lila Empson
Associate Editor: Janice Jacobson
Project Manager: Tom Dean
Manuscript written and prepared by Jan Coleman
Design: Whisner Design Group

Printed in China. All rights reserved under International Copyright Law. Contents and/or cover may not be reproduced in whole or in part in any form without the express written consent of the Publisher.

03 04/HK/ 4 3

Soul Retreats™
for Women

inspirio™

Contents

1. Today's Gift 8
2. Serenade the Soul 12
3. Master Plan 16
4. Trivial Pursuits 20
5. Cat Nap 24
6. Treasure Chest 28
7. Pamper Yourself 32
8. Chance It 36
9. Excellence, Not Perfection 40
10. Turning Pages 44
11. Tomorrow Is Another Day 48
12. Rose-Colored Glasses 52
13. Signed and Numbered 56
14. Security Guard 60
15. Quiet Corners 64

16. Reserved for You...68

17. Feminine Magic 72

18. Renew an Old Friendship...............................76

19. The Boomerang of Love 80

20. Through a Child's Eyes..................................84

21. Crowd out Worry...88

22. Beauty in the Ordinary...................................92

23. A Grateful Heart...96

24. Chuckle a Day...100

25. Just Enough 104

26. Roll with the Flow 108

27. Heaven's Stairs 112

28. It's a Wonderful Life.....................................116

29. Memory's Attic 120

30. Open Hands..124

Introduction

Like most women your life is busy—every day hums with activity. You dash at a full gallop through your day; you have lists to check off, meals to plan, errands to run, loved ones to care for. Wouldn't it be nice to slip away for a short break, a weekend retreat? It's not often possible, even when your body and soul yearn for restoring rest.

Soul Retreats™ for Women is the perfect solution. Set aside a few minutes in your day to pause for a deep breath, to refresh your mind with an inspiring word, and to withdraw into a snug place where your soul can be renewed.

Find your favorite chair, pour a comforting cup of tea, and settle in to your own Soul Retreat™. As you dwell in the beauty of the heavenly perspective, you'll be reminded of all God has in store for you right now.

Slow Me Down Lord

Slow me down, Lord, amid the confusion of my day.

Ease the rushing of my steps by the hushing of my heart.

Draw me in as I cast anchor to repair and restore.

Help me to remember that happiness is not a pursuit

toward an end, a place to finally arrive.

It comes as I spend a few moments a day

reflecting on the things that make my soul thrive.

Jan Coleman

Today's Gift

A Moment to Pause

Try getting up before daybreak. See the dawn emerge like a chorus in the morning twilight. You'll hear it whisper, *Today is a gift to you.* As you watch for that soaring burst of sun, let the serene beauty of that simple moment be stored in your soul.

The sun has been called the "eye of heaven," and its rising each day proclaims the glory of creation and symbolizes new life. Each time the sun peeks above the horizon, it brings a fresh promise—the gift of another day. Greet the day by beginning it well.

Develop a routine for getting up in the morning—your personally designed "order of the day." Wake up a little early, brew a special cup of tea or flavored coffee, and, before it gets hectic, spend a few moments in anticipation of what this day might bring. Seek the quiet comfort of a renewed heart and be thankful for the gift of today.

Each day comes bearing gifts,
Untie the ribbons.
—Ann Ruth Schabacker

A Moment to Reflect

God has given you today, this twenty-four hours, a block of time carved specifically for you. Nobody else will have a day like yours. You will have a few frustrations, but you will also have enriching joys, hopes, and invitations that you won't want to miss.

God is merciful to lift the curtain on each day with a new dawn. With it comes inspiration and renewed strength. Be encouraged this day with the moments God has given you. Let him show you the true value of time and how to enjoy it. Happiness is yours today.

When dawn breaks up another night,
And sunshine splits the dark with light;
My God, I pray with renewed heart,
Thank you for a brand-new start.

Each morning when my day is new,
Dear Lord, I place my trust in you;
Then all the worries on my mind,
Soon disappear, and peace I find.

—Sylvia Lavallée

*This is the day the LORD has made;
let us rejoice and be glad in it.*

Psalm 118:24

A Moment to Refresh

*The heavens are telling the glory of God;
and the firmament proclaims his handiwork.*

Psalm 19:1 NRSV

*Let the morning bring me word of your
unfailing love, LORD,
for I have put my trust in you.
Show me the way I should go,
for to you I lift up my soul.*

Psalm 143:8

*In the morning, O LORD, you hear my voice;
in the morning I lay my requests before you
and wait in expectation.*

Psalm 5:3

*Yesterday is a canceled check, and tomorrow is
a promissory note. But today is cash, ready for
us to spend in living.*

Barbara Johnson

*Normal day, let me be aware of the treasure you are.
Let me learn from you, love you, savor you, bless you
before I depart. Let me not pass by you in quest of
some rare and perfect tomorrow. Let me hold you
while I may for it will not always be so.*

—Mary Jean Irion

*One generation will commend your works
to another; they will tell of your mighty acts.
They will speak of the glorious splendor
of your majesty, and I will meditate on
your wonderful works, O Lord.*

Psalm 145:4–5

*Light is sweet,
and it pleases the eyes to see the sun.
However many years a man may live,
let him enjoy them all.*

Ecclesiastes 11:7–8

*The path of the righteous is like the first
gleam of dawn,
shining ever brighter till the full light of day.*

Proverbs 4:18

*Time is a precious
gift of God; so
precious that he only
gives it to us
moment by
moment.*

—Amelia Edith Barr

Serenade the Soul

A Moment to Pause

Stop a moment and listen to a bird as it warbles and chirps. You'll hear the voice of nature, the sound of music in its purest form. On the fifth day of creation, God said, "Let the birds increase on the earth." Could it be that he wanted the world to have music from the very start?

Music and song have an incredible charm and magic. They can calm an agitated heart and fill the soul with delight. What kind of music do you enjoy? A classical piece, a traditional hymn? Maybe you're prone to a lively country ditty, a good jazz ensemble, or the more contemporary sound. Perhaps lyrics or tunes sometimes float in your memory for days after hearing them because the music has touched you in a deep and profound way.

Pop in a tape or CD right now, or simply listen to the song of a bird. Let the music soothe you and fill your soul with delight. Bathe yourself in the music as it lifts and revives your spirit.

Next to theology, I give to music the highest place and honor. Music is the art of the prophets, the only art that can calm the agitation of the soul; it is one of the most magnificent and delightful presents God has given us.
—Martin Luther

A Moment to Reflect

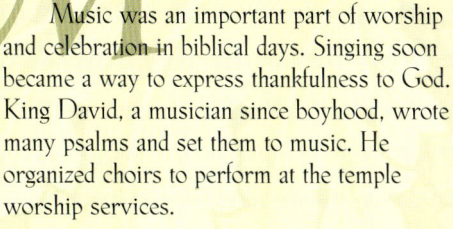

Music was an important part of worship and celebration in biblical days. Singing soon became a way to express thankfulness to God. King David, a musician since boyhood, wrote many psalms and set them to music. He organized choirs to perform at the temple worship services.

Music is one of God's greatest gifts, so bathe yourself in the music you love. Think of God as the great conductor, the ultimate musician. Music and worship fit naturally together. Let music lift your thoughts and emotions to God. The next time you enjoy your favorite music, thank God for it. Ask him to speak to you through a song, a hymn, or one of nature's melodies.

And the night shall be filled with music,
And the cares that infest the day,
Shall fold their tents like the Arabs,
And as silently steal away.

—Henry Wadsworth Longfellow

LORD, you are like a shield that keeps me safe. You help me win the battle. Your strong right hand keeps me going. You bend down to make me great.

Psalm 18:35 NIV

A Moment to Refresh

*Shout joyfully to the LORD, all the earth;
Break forth and sing for joy and sing praises.
Sing praises to the LORD with the lyre,
With the lyre and the sound of melody.
With trumpets and the sound of the horn
Shout joyfully before the King, the LORD.*

Psalm 98:4-6 NASB

Sing praises to the LORD, O you his faithful ones, and give thanks to his holy name.

Psalm 30:4 NRSV

Sing and make music in your heart to the Lord.

Ephesians 5:19

David told the leaders of the Levites to appoint their brothers as singers to sing joyful songs, accompanied by musical instruments: lyres, harps and cymbals.
1 Chronicles 15:16

*Music is God's best gift to man,
The only art of heaven given to earth,
The only art of earth we take to heaven.*

—Letitia Elizabeth Landon

*Sing to God, sing praises to his name;
lift up a song to him who rides upon the
clouds—his name is the* LORD—
be exultant before him.

Psalm 68:4 NRSV

The LORD *is my strength and my song;
he has become my salvation.
He is my God, and I will praise him,
my father's God, and I will exalt him.*

Exodus 15:2

*My heart is steadfast, O God;
I will sing and make music with all my
soul.*

Psalm 108:1

*Sing for joy to God our strength; shout
aloud to the God of Jacob! Begin the music,
strike the tambourine, play the melodious
harp and lyre.*

Psalm 81:1–2

*Who among us has
not sought peace in
a song?*

—Victor Hugo

Master Plan

A Moment to Pause   Sit back in your favorite chair and reflect on the events of the day. Did you receive a comforting hug, a word of encouragement, or a new insight you hadn't expected? These are no chance encounters, only God-arranged pieces of his master plan for you. Ordinary encounters that appear as coincidences are really God's loving hand on your life.

We don't usually see God's overall plan. Wouldn't it be great if our story were part of a feature film and the plot line mapped out in detail? We'd have specific directives for what to do, and we could avoid painful detours. Life, however, is more like a series of short vignettes, which purposes may be hidden for the moment.

In time, your life will be revealed and understood. You will be able to look back and see how your experiences fit together like a perfectly crafted puzzle. But for now, God wants only your willingness to agree to his plan in the slow and mysterious ways he sets it in motion. Whenever you feel anxious, just review God's promises and tuck them in your heart. God's plans for you are good.

"I know the plans I have for you," declares the LORD, "plans to prosper you and not to harm you, plans to give you hope and a future."
—Jeremiah 29:11

A Moment to Reflect

When you remind yourself every day that nothing is by chance with God, it calms the heart. Trusting that he is completely in charge of every detail can give you relief from burdens you need not carry.

Look at every situation, even the difficult ones, as an instrument for God to use for your ultimate good. Don't miss seeing God encourage you through a faithful friend or teach you through a stranger. Say in your heart, *That's you, God, isn't it?* You'll be astounded at the innumerable ways in which you see him craft his master plan.

When you're cast about by the storms of life,
When your days are filled with doubt or strife,
When nothing makes sense, it's hard to stand,
Remember this—God has a plan.

God has a plan, keep clinging to this,
Forget your agenda, look to his.
As you walk by faith, cling to his hand,
Remember this, God has a plan.

—Jan McIntosh

*All the ways of the LORD are loving and faithful
for those who keep the demands of his covenant.*
Psalm 25:10

A Moment to Refresh

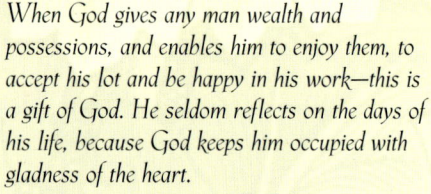

When God gives any man wealth and possessions, and enables him to enjoy them, to accept his lot and be happy in his work—this is a gift of God. He seldom reflects on the days of his life, because God keeps him occupied with gladness of the heart.
Ecclesiastes 5:19-20

Since the day we heard about you, we have not stopped praying for you and asking God to fill you with the knowledge of his will through all spiritual wisdom and understanding. And we pray this in order that you may live a life worthy of the Lord and may please him in every way: bearing fruit in every good work, growing in the knowledge of God.
Colossians 1:9-10

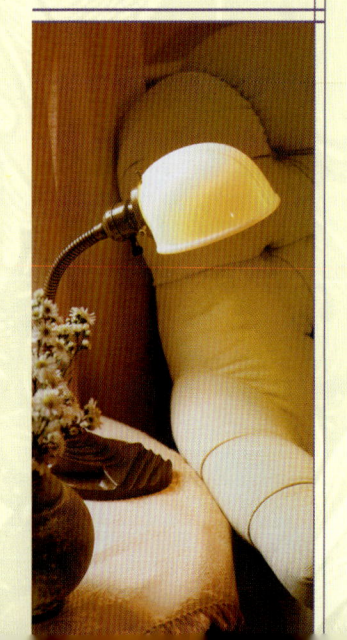

Perhaps you've been pondering your future plans and feel perplexed. Just remember Moses, who went from the pond, to the palace, to the pasture, to the pinnacle, to view the promised land before entering paradise. Praise the Lord!

—Patsy Clairmont

"I make known the end from the beginning, from ancient times what is still to come. I say: My purpose will stand, and I will do all that I please," says the Lord.

Isaiah 46:10

There is a time for everything, and a season for every activity under heaven.

Ecclesiastes 3:1

God who began a good work in you will carry it on to completion until the day of Christ Jesus.

Philippians 1:6

In all things God works for the good of those who love him, who have been called according to his purpose.

Romans 8:28

When we are rightly related to God, life is full of spontaneous joyful uncertainty and expectancy. We do not know what God is going to do next; he packs our life with surprises.

—Oswald Chambers

Trivial Pursuits

A Moment to Pause

Are you overextended and dashing in different directions? Do you often feel like a sock tossing around in the dryer? Does there always seem to be another objective, another goal, another task, another commitment? Are your priorities a constant juggle? Yes? Sit down with a pencil, find a quiet corner, and start making a list. Title it "trivial pursuits."

Ask yourself: What things that don't really count take up my precious time? Do I neglect the relationships that really matter? Do I spend time on things that nurture my soul, please God, and enhance my relationship with him?

Identify the nonessential drains on your time and plan to trim them from your life.

Bring balance and order to your life by spending time on activities that will help you be a whole person and by seeking fulfillment in God's purpose in everything you do.

Tell me to what you pay attention, and I will tell you who you are.
—José Ortega y Gasset

A Moment to Reflect

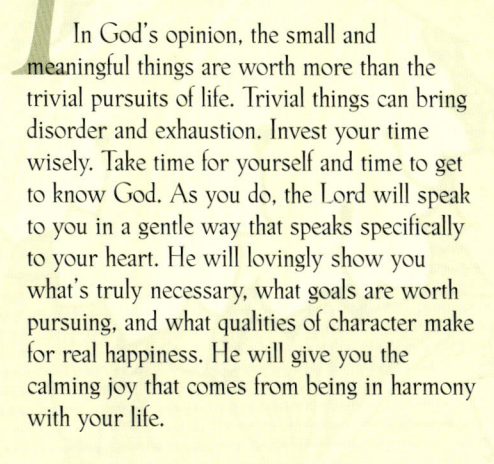

In God's opinion, the small and meaningful things are worth more than the trivial pursuits of life. Trivial things can bring disorder and exhaustion. Invest your time wisely. Take time for yourself and time to get to know God. As you do, the Lord will speak to you in a gentle way that speaks specifically to your heart. He will lovingly show you what's truly necessary, what goals are worth pursuing, and what qualities of character make for real happiness. He will give you the calming joy that comes from being in harmony with your life.

Earthly treasures won't stand the test,
For in time, moth and rust will destroy.
Come with me, to your place of rest,
In my presence, there's fullness of joy.

A shelter where trials of life will cease,
Through the comfort of my love divine.
Where I quietly whisper into the peace,
"I am yours, won't you please be mine"?

—Sylvia Lavallée

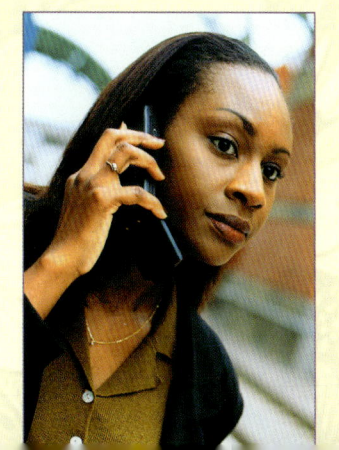

*Seek first his kingdom and his righteousness,
and all these things will be given to you as well.*

Matthew 6:33

A Moment to Refresh

Do not store up for yourselves treasures on earth, where moth and rust destroy, and where thieves break in and steal. But store up for yourselves treasures in heaven, where moth and rust do not destroy, and where thieves do not break in and steal. For where your treasure is, there your heart will be also.

Matthew 6:19-21

*Turn my heart toward your statues
and not toward selfish gain.
Turn my eyes away from worthless things;
preserve my life according to your word.*

Psalm 119:36-37

All those things that I might count as profit I now reckon as loss for Christ's sake. Not only those things; I reckon everything as complete loss for the sake of what is so much more valuable, the knowledge of Jesus Christ my Lord.

Philippians 3:7-8 GNT

Take glory in neither money, if you have some, nor in influential friends, but in God who gives you everything and above all wants to give you himself.

—Thomas à Kempis

Martha was distracted by all the preparations that had to be made. She came to Jesus and asked, "Lord, don't you care that my sister has left me to do the work by myself? Tell her to help me!" "Martha, Martha," the Lord answered, "you are worried and upset about many things, but only one thing is needed. Mary has chosen what is better, and it will not be taken away from her."

Luke 10:40–42

A good name is to be more desired than great wealth,
Favor is better than silver and gold.

Proverbs 22:1 NASB

Your beauty should consist of your true inner self, the ageless beauty of a gentle and quiet spirit, which is of the greatest value in God's sight.

1 Peter 3:4 GNT

At the end of life, you will never regret not having passed one more test, not winning one more verdict, not closing one more deal. You will regret time not spent with a husband, a child, a friend, a parent.

—Barbara Bush

Cat Nap

A Moment to Pause

Do you sometimes feel like you can't get enough sleep? You're going full tilt and can't get the rest you need? If only you could grab a little nap? Don't feel guilty; resting is not selfish. Renewal isn't a convenience reserved for a lady of leisure, it's a "must do" if you want to stay stable and sane in today's world. Reward yourself with slumber. It can be one of the best things you can do for body and soul.

The best time for a nap is when you're on the run and have no time. Don't wait for exhaustion to overtake you—find a quiet spot for a thirty-minute nap. Fold your hands over your chest, close your eyes, breathe deeply, and drift off. Leave worries and concerns outside the gates of dreamland.

Sleep restores and regenerates. Remember the story of Sleeping Beauty? After pricking her finger on the spinning wheel, she fell into a long, deep sleep, but after a prince's kiss she woke up more beautiful than ever, to a life of promise and hope. Sleep is where God touches the depths of the soul with a caring hand.

I will lie down and sleep in peace,
for you alone, O LORD,
make me dwell in safety.
—Psalm 4:8

A Moment to Reflect

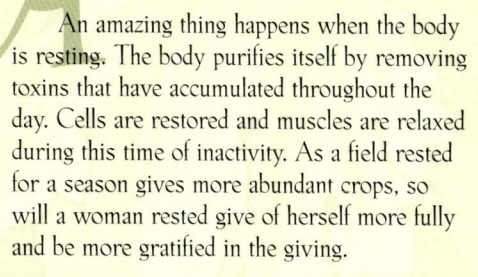

An amazing thing happens when the body is resting. The body purifies itself by removing toxins that have accumulated throughout the day. Cells are restored and muscles are relaxed during this time of inactivity. As a field rested for a season gives more abundant crops, so will a woman rested give of herself more fully and be more gratified in the giving.

There are many scriptures in the Bible that refer to sleep and rest. Even God rested from his work to demonstrate how important it is. So enjoy a short siesta. As you sleep, God will soothe your weariness. His wisdom will gently filter through your quiet mind. When you wake, you'll have more energy to be your best.

Sleep is the celestial nurse who croons away our consciousness, and God deals with the unconscious life of the soul in places where only he and his angels have charge. As you retire to rest, give your soul and God a time together, and commit your life to God with a conscious peace for the hours of sleep.

—Oswald Chambers

*Be at rest once more, O my soul,
for the LORD has been good to you.*

         Psalm 116:7

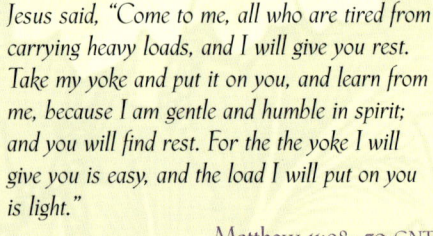

A Moment to Refresh

Jesus said, "Come to me, all who are tired from carrying heavy loads, and I will give you rest. Take my yoke and put it on you, and learn from me, because I am gentle and humble in spirit; and you will find rest. For the the yoke I will give you is easy, and the load I will put on you is light."

         Matthew 11:28–30 GNT

*I lie down and sleep;
I wake again, because the LORD sustains me.*

         Psalm 3:5

"I will refresh the weary and satisfy the faint," says the Lord.

         Jeremiah 31:25

The LORD makes me lie down in green pastures, he leads me beside quiet waters, he restores my soul.

         Psalm 23:2–3

O bed! O bed! delicious bed!
That heaven upon earth to the weary head.

—Thomas Hood

By the seventh day God had finished the work he had been doing; so on the seventh day he rested from all his work. And God blessed the seventh day and made it holy, because on it he rested from all the work of creating that he had done.
Genesis 2:2–3

Solomon stood and blessed the whole assembly of Israel in a loud voice, saying: "Praise be to the LORD, who has given rest to his people Israel just as he promised. Not one word has failed of all the good promises he gave through his servant Moses."
1 Kings 8:55–56

Anyone who enters God's rest also rests from his own work, just as God did from his.
Hebrews 4:10

"Holy leisure" refers to a sense of balance in life, an ability to be at peace throughout the activities of the day, an ability to rest and take time to enjoy beauty, an ability to pace ourselves.

—Richard Foster

Treasure Chest

A Moment to Pause

Look around your home. What are the things you most treasure? The things you display with great care? What items would you want to protect if your house was burning? Think back to the last time you visited a museum. Remember the collections displayed? Museums are full of an assortment of rare books, precious one-of-a-kind documents, relics from past centuries or ancient civilizations that are considered important and worth saving.

Imagine the people filing past many of these fragile objects, some enclosed in glass. You hear a respectful hush in the room, a sense of awe at the treasures in view, a realization that these things are one of a kind and beyond monetary value. You leave knowing that you've been privileged to see these priceless treasures. You are grateful that these items are being preserved for generations to come.

Whenever you find your self-esteem wilting, envision this scene, and remember that you, too, are priceless—to God. He will go to great lengths to preserve and sustain you. You are his treasure—the best of his collection—and you are of immeasurable value to him.

The human soul is God's treasury, out of which he coins unspeakable riches. Thoughts and feelings, desires and yearnings, faith and hope—these are the most precious things that God finds in us.
—Henry Ward Beecher

A Moment to Reflect

If you consider yourself a treasure to the Lord, you can comprehend more of his depth and richness. The more you understand how much you are worth to God, the more cherished and accepted you will feel. What a revelation! Regardless of your shortcomings, the Lord paid the highest price imaginable for you. Your weight in gold? Your weight in sacrificing love.

You have a God who knows you thoroughly, who values every facet of you, who knows how to bring out your very best. Allow him access to your life. Let him show you off to the world, and others will see his goodness reflected through you.

Each precious soul is a living jewel
A treasure set apart for the Lord
To reflect through every facet of life
The eternal light of His Holy Word.

From dust each gem was created
Sealed with love for all eternity
To display to a world in darkness
God's crown jewels of victory.

—SYLVIA LAVALLÉE

The LORD has declared this day that you are his people, his treasured possession as he promised, and that you are to keep all his commands.

Deuteronomy 26:18

A Moment to Refresh

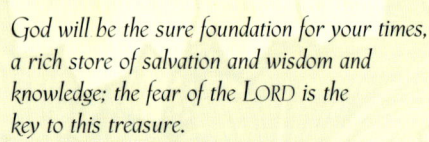

God will be the sure foundation for your times, a rich store of salvation and wisdom and knowledge; the fear of the LORD is the key to this treasure.

Isaiah 33:6

*When I consider your heavens,
the work of your fingers,
the moon and the stars,
which you have set in place,
what is man that you are mindful of him,
O LORD, the son of man that you care for him?
You made him a little lower than the heavenly beings and crowned him with glory and honor.*

Psalm 8:3–5

*Keep me as the apple of the eye;
Hide me in the shadow of Your wings, O Lord.*

Psalm 17:8 NASB

God does not love us because we are valuable.
We are valuable because God loves us.

—Archbishop Fulton Sheen

The LORD God is a sun and shield;
the LORD bestows favor and honor;
no good thing does he withhold
from those whose walk is blameless.

Psalm 84:11

LORD, you have assigned me my portion
and my cup; you have made my lot secure.
The boundary lines have fallen for me in
pleasant places; surely I have a
delightful inheritance.

Psalm 16:5–6

God, who said, "Let light shine out of
darkness," made his light shine in our
hearts to give us the light of the knowledge
of the glory of God in the face of Christ.
But we have this treasure in jars of clay to
show that this all-surpassing power is from
God and not from us.

2 Corinthians 4:6–7

You are God's dearly beloved and the object of His affection. The apple of His eye. Heir to His kingdom. He planned the redemption He makes real in you every day. When you respond by living your life with meaning, you reveal your commitment to the covenant between you and Him.

—Kari West

Pamper Yourself

A Moment to Pause

Find some time to pamper yourself. In Ecclesiastes, Solomon says to enjoy to the fullest the life that God has given. Recognize and enjoy the fruits of your labor as another of God's wonderful gifts. It is a good thing.

The dictionary defines pamper in this way: "to be indulgent with, to coddle, to spoil." As a woman, you may cringe at the thought of spoiling, of giving in too much to a child's impulses. You know that many a character has been ruined by a lenient parent. But you aren't a child; you are a woman. Occasional pampering can refresh and prepare you to meet the complex demands on your time.

So, how do you want to pamper yourself today? You could splurge on a new hairstyle or buy some real maple syrup for your pancakes. What about picking up that new outfit you looked at last week or treating yourself to a day out with some girlfriends for lunch and a movie? Indulge in something that will make you smile, make you stop and say, "Now, that was really worth it!"

The best thing a man can do is eat and drink and enjoy what we has earned. And yet, I realized that even this comes from God.
—Ecclesiastes 2:24 GNT

A Moment to Reflect

God wants to hold nothing back from you. He's pleased when you take time for yourself to buy something special or to have a little fun. He wants to express himself in all the enjoyable things that come your way. God wants to add to your inner beauty, your outer usefulness, and your gladness.

As you pamper yourself, your daily work has more meaning and purpose. It helps keep your world in better balance. God provides both work and pleasure as ways to serve him. Enjoy life to the fullest, and be constantly aware that all comes from his hand.

Live while you live, the Epicure would say,
And seize the pleasures of the present day;
Live while you live, the sacred preacher cries,
And give to God each moment as it flies;
Lord, in my view let both united be;
I live in pleasure when I live to thee.

—PHILLIP DODDRIDGE

*The Lord satisfies your desires with good things
so that your youth is renewed like the eagle's.*
Psalm 103:5

A Moment to Refresh

*From the fullness of his grace, we have all
received one blessing after another.*
John 1:16

*You have made known to me the path of life,
O Lord; you will fill me with joy
in your presence, with eternal pleasures
at your right hand.*
Psalm 16:11

The joy of the LORD is your strength.
Nehemiah 8:10

*The grace that is reaching more and more
people may cause thanksgiving to overflow to
the glory of God.*
1 Corinthians 4:15

Freedom means I have been set free to become all that God wants me to be, to achieve all that God wants me to achieve, to enjoy all that God wants me to enjoy.

—Warren Wiersbe

Praise the LORD, O My soul, and forget not all his benefits.

Psalm 103:2

His merciful kindness is great toward us: and the truth of the LORD endureth for ever. Praise ye the LORD.

Psalm 117:2 KJV

God has shown kindness by giving you rain from heaven and crops in their seasons; he provides you with plenty of food and fills your hearts with joy.

Acts 14:17

Jesus said, "I tell you the truth, my father will give you whatever you ask for in my name. Until now you have not asked for anything in my name. Ask and you will receive, and your joy will be complete."

John 16:23–24

I asked God for all things so I could enjoy life. He gave me life so I could enjoy all things.

—Author Unknown

Chance It

A Moment to Pause

Do you have dreams for the future, prospects you'd like to explore in your life? A new career, a home business, a challenging hobby? Is it hard for you to take steps into the unknown? Does an old fear knock on the door and cry *Forget it, you can't do it, it's out of your reach?*

Picture in your mind a pioneer woman on a great adventure across the plains to settle a new land in the west. Imagine her courage as she left comfort and security behind to venture forth, to be a part of settling a new and untamed land. She probably had a healthy dose of fear, too, but it didn't keep her from taking a chance.

Is there a pioneer inside of you? Talk to God today about pursuing your dreams. Ask him to go forward with you, to be at your side as you explore new regions in your life. Trust him to give you boldness and enthusiasm, to share the risks with you, to let you know which roads to take, which corners to turn. Say to yourself, *I can do it with God's help.*

God has not given us a spirit of timidity, but of power and love and discipline.
—2 Timothy 1:7 NASB

A Moment to Reflect

Confidence in God is essential for the pioneer. With faith comes the boldness you need. When you pursue the dreams he has placed in your heart, using the gifts and talents he's given you, there is no reason to fear. No dream is too big for him.

There will be setbacks and disappointments, and you'll want to look before you leap, but as someone said, the one who tries something and fails is much better off than the one who tries to do nothing and succeeds. Look ahead with hope and anticipation as you step out beyond your limitations. A solid faith in God and a willingness to take chances will clothe your dreams in reality.

Deep in every woman lies a vast frontier,
Horizons to explore, dream-wagons to steer.
As in the past, those days of old,
The way is dusty and sometimes cold.

When clouds of doubt should appear
Know you are made for faith, not fear.
You must find your way, be bold enough to dare,
With provision from the Lord and security in prayer.

—Jan Coleman

Be strong and let your heart take courage,
*All you who hope in the L*ORD.
									Psalm 31:24 NASB

A Moment to Refresh

May God give you the desire of your heart
and make all your plans succeed.
									Psalm 20:4

*Delight yourself in the L*ORD
and he will give you the desires of your heart.
									Psalm 37:4

Do not fear for I am with you;
do not be dismayed, for I am your God.
									Isaiah 41:10

Such confidence as this is ours through Christ
before God. Not that we are competent in
ourselves to claim anything for ourselves, but
our competence comes from God.
									2 Corinthians 3:4–5

*We are all faced with a series of great opportunities
brilliantly disguised as impossible situations.*

—CHARLES SWINDOLL

*When I called, you answered me;
you made me bold and stouthearted,
O LORD.*

Psalm 138:3

*May the God of hope fill you with all joy
and peace as you trust in him, so that you
may overflow with hope by the power of the
Holy Spirit.*

Romans 15:13

*Many are the plans in a man's heart,
but it is the LORD'S purpose that prevails.*

Proverbs 19:21

*In him and through faith in him we may
approach God with freedom and confidence.*

Ephesians 3:12

*Mountain-moving
faith is not just
dreaming and
desiring. It is daring
to risk failure.*

—MARY KAY ASH

Excellence, Not Perfection

A Moment to Pause

Take a quiet walk through your neighborhood or a nearby park. Let the gentle wind and rustle of the leaves quiet your heart. Then take some time to ponder this question: "Do I strive for perfection in my life?" Perhaps you don't strive for perfection all the time, but are there some areas of your life where you feel that you are not quite good enough? Where you just don't measure up to what you "should" be? Do you keep trying harder to be a better woman, but your efforts never seem to be good enough? Does it seem that somebody keeps moving the mark on the measuring stick a few notches higher? (Now, who could that be?)

Striving for perfection is an impossible quest; perfection is a myth and forever out of reach. Aim for excellence, instead. Excellence has nothing to do with outward appearances or with what you accomplish or with what you possess. Excellence depends solely on what you are from God's perspective—and God doesn't focus on your flaws.

When you seek God's ideal, you will throw away your measuring stick. You don't need one that marks success and quality of life by the world's standards. Christ requires only simplicity of heart.

What is Christian perfection? Loving God with
all our heart, mind, soul, and strength.
—John Wesley

A Moment to Reflect

God judges a woman by her character, by what she pursues in her life. As you ponder this, ask God to draw out all that is excellent in you. Let him shape you with faithfulness, honor, and integrity. Be aware of how he adds these finishing touches on your life in a way that will give glory to him and the greatest satisfaction and meaning for you.

Be ready to radiate from the inside out. Don't be surprised when you're asked, "Tell me, where did you get your great new look?" Outward change will be perceptible but subtle—a glow to the skin, a sparkle in the eye, a tilt of the head, a lilt to the walk—but you'll know the inward change makes the difference.

If you check out the life of Jesus you will discover what made him perfect. He did not attain a state of perfection by carrying around in his pocket a list of rules and regulations, or by seeking to conform to the cultural mores of the time. He was perfect because he never made a move without his Father.

—TOM SKINNER

*Blessed are you, O L*ORD*;
teach me your statutes.*

Psalm 119:12 NRSV

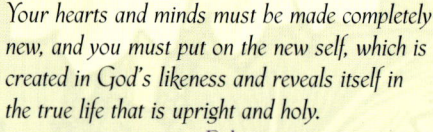

A Moment to Refresh

Your hearts and minds must be made completely new, and you must put on the new self, which is created in God's likeness and reveals itself in the true life that is upright and holy.

Ephesians 4:23–24 GNT

*Show me your ways, O L*ORD
*teach me your paths
guide me in your truth and teach me,
for you are God my Savior,
and my hope is in you all day long.*

Psalm 25:4–5

God said, "People look at the outward appearance, but I look at the heart."

1 Samuel 16:7 GNT

There is nothing you can do to make God love you more. There is nothing you can do to make God love you less. His love is unconditional, impartial, everlasting, infinite, perfect. God is love!

—AUTHOR UNKNOWN

Let us fix our eyes on Jesus, the author and perfecter of our faith, who for the joy set before him endured the cross, scorning its shame, and sat down at the right hand of the throne of God.

Hebrews 12:2

I press on toward the goal to win the prize for which God has called me heavenward in Christ Jesus.

Philippians 3:14

Teach me to do your will, for you are my God; may your good Spirit lead me on level ground.

Psalm 143:10

Of all classes and descriptions of persons on this earth, they are the happiest of whom it may be said that the things most hoped for by them are the things not seen.

—MENNONITE WRITINGS

Turning Pages

A Moment to Pause

Treat yourself to something good to read today, a book that seems alive, a story that speaks right to you, one that is so gripping and the characters so appealing that you're a bit sad when you come to the end. It feels like you're saying good-bye to a friend.

It's been said that a good book contains more wealth than a good bank, and that a drop of ink can make a million people think. Curl up with something delicious to read. Select something that transports you to another time and another place, that makes you laugh, or that brings you to tears with a poignant scene. Maybe you prefer books or magazines that challenge your mind, make you examine theories, or teach lessons for life. Whatever your preference, set aside time to soak in some words.

What you read will inspire, inform, and delight you. It will calm your spirit when you need it the most. A good book is like an afternoon in a fragrant garden. Just knowing that a good book is waiting at the end of your long day can make the anticipation so much the sweeter.

A book is like a garden carried in the pocket.
—Ancient Proverb

A Moment to Reflect

Whatever you read for pleasure, take time to nourish your soul with God's word. He's written a book of letters just for you, packed with wisdom and truth. His book is full of answers to your questions and promises for your future. If a problem or situation eludes a solution, ask God to direct you to his answer for you. Keep your heart attuned to God's good desire for your life, and read prayerfully.

God's words will nourish you long after you close the book. Stow your favorite passages away in your heart. They'll cleanse your emotions, enlighten your mind, and wrap you in confirming love.

I love old books
Frayed from pages turning.
Their warm, soft binding,
The words deftly planned.
They lead me through a story
Like a dear friend's hand.

—JAN COLEMAN

Be not conformed to this world: but be ye transformed by the renewing of your mind, that ye may prove what is that good, and acceptable, and perfect, will of God.

Romans 12:2 KJV

A Moment to Refresh

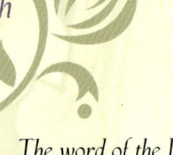

The word of the LORD is right and true; he is faithful in all he does.

Psalm 33:4

Wisdom is sweet to your soul; if you find it, there is a future hope for you, and your hope will not be cut off.

Proverbs 24:14

The wisdom that comes from heaven is first of all pure; then peace-loving, considerate, submissive, full of mercy and good fruit, impartial and sincere.

James 3:17

I will remember the deeds of the Lord; yes, I will remember your miracles of long ago. I will meditate on all your works and consider all your mighty deeds.

Psalm 77:11–12

Next to acquiring good friends, the best acquisition is that of a good book.

—Charles Caleb Colton

How much better it is to get wisdom than gold! And to get understanding is to be chosen above silver.
Proverbs 16:16 NASB

The sayings of the wise are like the sharp sticks that shepherds use to guide sheep, and collected proverbs are as lasting as firmly driven nails. They have been given by God, the one Shepherd of us all.
Ecclesiastes 12:11 GNT

I rejoice in following your statues as one who rejoices in great riches, O Lord. I meditate on your precepts and consider your ways.
Psalm 119:14–15

A single line in the Bible has consoled me more than all the books I've ever read.

—Immanuel Kant

Tomorrow Is Another Day

A Moment to Pause

Gone with the Wind, an unforgettable story by Margaret Mitchell, sold more than fifty thousand copies on the first day of its release in 1936. Scarlett O'Hara, a fiery young southern belle with the world at her plantation doorstep, encounters a war that changes her country and her life. She emerges strong and determined, but due to a misplaced dream and some hasty and foolish decisions, Scarlett misses her chance at true happiness.

Why has this story captured the minds of millions? Is it the struggle of a society to rise from the ashes of destruction, or is it the immortal hope expressed by Scarlett in the last line of the book, "After all, tomorrow is another day"?

Most people have regrets of failures and missed opportunities. That's why stories like Scarlett's have such timeless appeal. There is a need for a refuge like Tara to examine one's life, lick one's wounds, learn one's lessons, and have another chance to make things right, where endings are happy, dreams come true, and Rhett comes home.

It's never too late—in fiction or in life—to revise.
—Nancy Thayer

A Moment to Reflect

Whenever your failures fly through your mind, keep in mind that failure is not the same as defeat in God's plan. What could seem like an ending may really be a new beginning, for God gives second chances. God uses your fumbles to redirect your life, remold your goals, and reveal your priorities. He'll renew your spirit and make you ready for triumph and happiness.

The name Tara refers to a hill in ancient Ireland, the royal seat of the Celtic high kings. When you're discouraged, just retreat to your own Tara, your heavenly Father's arms, and let his gentle hand steal over your heart. His love can grant you a fresh start.

Things in the past,
Are dead and gone,
Leave them behind,
Then just move on.

Yesterday is history,
Tomorrow is a mystery,
Today is God's gift to me,
To make it all that it can be.

—SYLVIA LAVALLÉE

If anyone is in Christ, he is a new creation; the old has gone, the new has come!

2 Corinthians 5:17

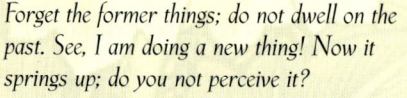

A Moment to Refresh

Forget the former things; do not dwell on the past. See, I am doing a new thing! Now it springs up; do you not perceive it?

Isaiah 43:18–19

This I call to mind and therefore I have hope: Because of the LORD's great love we are not consumed, for his compassions never fail. They are new every morning; great is your faithfulness.

Lamentations 3:21–23

Happy are those who...find joy in obeying the Law of the Lord, and they study it day and night. They are like trees that grow beside a stream, that bear fruit at the right time, and whose leaves do not dry up. They succeed in everything they do.

Psalm 1:1–3 GNT

What becomes of lost opportunities? Perhaps our guardian angel gathers them up and will give them back when we've grown wiser—and will use them rightly.

—HELEN KELLER

Whatever you do, work at it with all your heart, as working for the Lord, not for men, since you know that you will receive an inheritance from the Lord as a reward. It is the Lord Christ you are serving.
Colossians 3:23–24

Instead of their shame my people will receive a double portion, and instead of disgrace they will rejoice in their inheritance; and so they will inherit a double portion in their land, and everlasting joy will be theirs.
Isaiah 61:7

You will surely forget your trouble, recalling it only as waters gone by.
Job 11:16

You have been my hope, O Sovereign LORD, *my confidence since my youth.*
Psalm 71:5

If you have made mistakes... there is always another chance for you. You may have a fresh start any moment you choose, for this thing we call "failure" is not the falling down, but the staying down.

—MARY PICKFORD

Rose-Colored Glasses

A Moment to Pause

Tuck this story into your memory. A gal who is remembered around the world for her mountainous hope was described as "being excessively cheerful and unduly optimistic." She was said to have looked at an impossible situation through rose-colored glasses.

Five days into a trip across the Atlantic on the legendary Titanic, Margaret Tobin Brown found herself bobbing around in a lifeboat in the freezing cold with fourteen other women and a prophet-of-doom officer. The officer insisted they'd never escape the undertow when the ship went down.

Margaret refused to give in to negative thinking. If this man wasn't going to save the lifeboat, she would. She insisted they keep warm by fast-paced rowing during those daunting hours before they were rescued, and lifted their hopes with her indomitable spirit. She created survivor lists and radioed them to the families. She even raised money for destitute victims of the sinking, collecting almost $10,000 in pledges. She rightly earned the famous nickname, "The Unsinkable Molly Brown."

Write a note on the refrigerator to remind you that with God all things are possible. Take a moment to thank God for his gift of rose-colored glasses. Feel your spirit lift immediately.

Your living is determined not so much by what life brings to you as by the attitude you bring to life; not so much by what happens to you as by the way your mind looks at what happens. Circumstances and situations do color life, but you.... choose what the color will be.
—John Homer Miller

A Moment to Reflect

If you're uncertain about something today and find yourself slipping into negative thinking, make a point to zero in on the positive. If you can't see through the fog, if your future is fuzzy, it's a great opportunity to practice being optimistic.

If you're overwhelmed with doubt, remember that God wants to give you a buoyant spirit to rise above any circumstance, no matter how difficult. When you place your confidence in God, you are secure in the hope of your Savior. With him at your side, you, too, will be unsinkable.

The more faith you have,
The more you believe,
The more goals you set
The more you'll achieve.

....

Remember no matter
How futile things seem,
With faith, there is no
Impossible dream!

—ALICE JOYCE DAVIDSON

Whatever is true, whatever is noble, whatever is right, whatever is pure, whatever is lovely, whatever is admirable—if anything is excellent or praiseworthy—think about such things.
Philippians 4:8

A Moment to Refresh

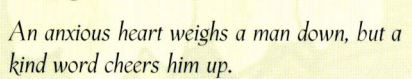

An anxious heart weighs a man down, but a kind word cheers him up.
Proverbs 12:25

We wait in hope for the LORD; he is our help and our shield. In him our hearts rejoice, for we trust in his holy name. May your unfailing love rest upon us, O LORD, even as we put our hope in you.
Psalm 33:20–22

Great is your love, reaching to the heavens; your faithfulness reaches to the skies.
Psalm 57:10

A cheerful heart is good medicine.
Proverbs 17:22

A happy person is not a person in a certain set of circumstances, but rather a person with a certain set of attitudes.

—Hugh Downs

Love always protects, always trusts, always hopes, always perseveres. Love never fails.
1 Corinthians 13:7–8

Give thanks to the LORD, call on his name; make known among the nations what he has done. Sing to him, sing praise to him; tell of all his wonderful acts. Glory in his holy name; let the hearts of those who seek the LORD rejoice. Look to the LORD and his strength; seek his face always.
1 Chronicles 16:8–11

Whatever you do, work at it with all your heart, as working for the Lord.
Colossians 3:23

The way in which you endure that which you must endure is more important than the crisis itself.

—Sam Rutigliano

Signed and Numbered

A Moment to Pause

Thomas Kinkade is a world-renowned artist known as the "painter of light." Raised in a simple home in a small town in the California foothills, Kinkade developed a unique style of making the images he paints glow from within. As a young man, he earned his living selling originals in local galleries. His art grew in popularity until it became a phenomenon unprecedented in recent times.

The paintings were made into limited edition prints that mushroomed in value because they were signed and numbered by the artist. Kinkade's captivating scenes affirm the basic values of family and home, faith in God, and the radiant beauty of the Lord's creation. Kinkade credits God with his ability and success.

Think of a piece of art you admire, and pretend you are the artist at the moment of inspiration, about to paint a masterpiece that will bring joy and comfort to many. That's the way God designed you. You are an original, a unique portrait, unlike any other piece of art that God has ever made.

Creativity is one of the great privileges of being human. You apply hands and mind and spirit to fashion something that did not exist before in that precise form. You touch the universe with your own unique personality and somehow at least a little corner of the universe is changed.
—*Thomas Kinkade*

A Moment to Reflect

The Bible says that God created you, that he was pleased to make you his own, and that he summons you by name. Take a moment to bask in the thought that you are an original, signed and numbered by the Master's own hand.

Before you were born he sketched a design of undetermined value—you. You are the only one just like you. You are number one; there is no number two or number three. You are so much more than a limited edition—you are an exclusive edition. Your inner character and your special personality are evidence that you are truly one of a kind.

We master fear through faith—faith in the worthwhileness of life and the trustworthiness of God; faith in the meaning of our pain and our striving, and confidence that God will not cast us aside but will use each one of us as a piece of priceless mosaic in the design of his universe.

—JOSHUA LOTH LIEBMAN

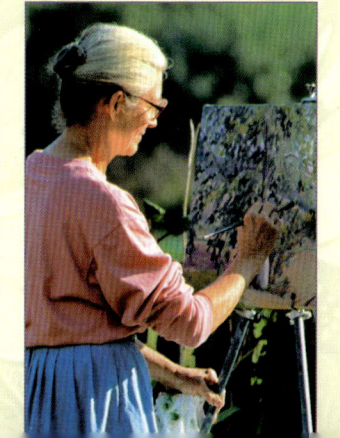

You created every part of me; you put me together in my mother's womb.

Psalm 139:13 GNT

A Moment to Refresh

The LORD is good to all; he has compassion on all he has made.

Psalm 145:9

Know that the LORD is God. It is he who made us, and we are his; we are his people, the sheep of his pasture.

Psalm 100:3

He has predestined us to adoption as sons through Jesus Christ to Himself, according to the kind intention of His will.

Ephesians 1:5 NASB

Sixty queens there may be, and eighty concubines, and virgins beyond number; but my dove, my perfect one, is unique.

Song of Solomon 6:8–9

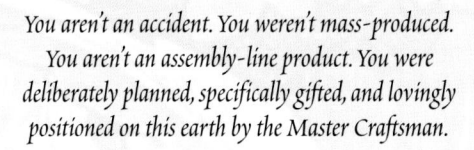

You aren't an accident. You weren't mass-produced. You aren't an assembly-line product. You were deliberately planned, specifically gifted, and lovingly positioned on this earth by the Master Craftsman.

—MAX LUCADO

Arise, shine, for your light has come, and the glory of the LORD rises upon you.
Isaiah 60:1

You are a chosen people, a royal priesthood, a holy nation, a people belonging to God, that you may declare the praises of him who called you out of darkness into his wonderful light.
1 Peter 2:9

We are God's workmanship, created in Christ Jesus to do good works, which God prepared in advance for us to do.
Ephesians 2:10

How great is the love the Father has lavished on us, that we should be called children of God! And that is what we are!
1 John 3:1

Man is heaven's masterpiece.

—FRANCIS QUARLES

Security Guard

A Moment to Pause

When you see an officer in uniform on a street corner or a security guard at the shopping mall, do you get a sense of safety? Are you comforted simply by knowing someone is in charge and keeping watch?

In the early days of World War II, many people feared enemy attacks on North America. Home guards were created, and soon millions of volunteers, persons ineligible for military service because of age or medical condition, became air-raid wardens. They wore official uniforms—white metal helmets and a whistle—and patrolled the streets during air-raid drills. They were well trained for fire and medical emergencies as well. Having home guards in place to watch out for enemy planes or suspicious activity brought a sense of assurance to families during uncertain times.

Close your eyes and picture the Lord as your personal security guard. You have a watchman who always has his eyes peeled for danger. He is on constant surveillance in your life, and he is capable of handling any crisis that may come from any direction. He never leaves you unguarded.

In God's faithfulness lies eternal security.
—Corrie ten Boom

A Moment to Reflect

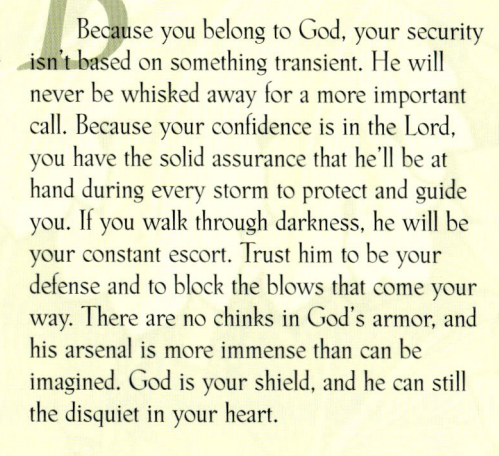

Because you belong to God, your security isn't based on something transient. He will never be whisked away for a more important call. Because your confidence is in the Lord, you have the solid assurance that he'll be at hand during every storm to protect and guide you. If you walk through darkness, he will be your constant escort. Trust him to be your defense and to block the blows that come your way. There are no chinks in God's armor, and his arsenal is more immense than can be imagined. God is your shield, and he can still the disquiet in your heart.

You're never alone with Jesus,
He's always at your side,
Giving strength and wisdom
With you, he will abide.
To keep you safe from danger
The trials that come your way
You're never alone with Jesus
He's with you every day

—Colette Fedor

You are my hiding place; you will protect me from trouble and surround me with songs of deliverance.

Psalm 32:7

A Moment to Refresh

The LORD is with me; he is my helper. I will look in triumph on my enemies. It is better to take refuge in the Lord than to trust in man.

Psalm 118:7–8

The LORD is my light and my salvation; whom shall I fear? the LORD is the strength of my life; of whom shall I be afraid?

Psalm 27:1 KJV

He will cover you with his feathers, and under his wings you will find refuge; his faithfulness will be your shield and rampart.

Psalm 91:4

LORD, you have assigned me my portion and my cup; you have made my lot secure.

Psalm 16:5

Angels guard you when you walk with Me. What better way could you choose?

—FRANCES J. ROBERTS

He will command his angels concerning you to guard you in all your ways.
Psalm 91:11

Have no fear of sudden disaster or of the ruin that overtakes the wicked, for the LORD *will be your confidence and will keep your foot from being snared.*
Proverbs 3:25–26

We have this hope as an anchor for the soul, firm and secure.
Hebrews 6:19

I will lie down and sleep in peace, for you alone, O LORD, *make me dwell in safety.*
Psalm 4:8

Protect me, my Lord, my boat is so small, and your ocean is so big.

—BRETON FISHERMAN'S PRAYER

Quiet Corners

A Moment to Pause

Do you long for a quiet corner? A place to get away from the outside world, to retreat from the overload of daily life—rush-hour traffic, insistent telephones, unending e-mail messages? You are not alone. Some women have discovered monasteries where guests can gain distance from the overload, eat simple meals in silence, stroll on winding trails through forest and canyon, contemplate, and pray. One visitor described it as a "detox center" for her soul.

A monastery retreat isn't always possible, but you can create your own private haven at home, an oasis where you can spend some downtime. Settle into a spot where you can relax your mind—a windswept beach, a shady garden, a comfortable chair on the front porch—and unwind after the rigors of the day.

Solitude can be your best companion. In the stillness of your heart, you can regenerate and renew.

Practice the art of aloneness and you will discover the treasure of tranquillity. Develop the art of solitude and you will unearth the gift of serenity.
—William Arthur Ward

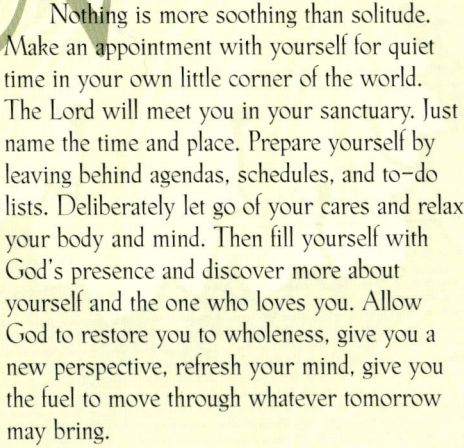

A Moment to Reflect

Nothing is more soothing than solitude. Make an appointment with yourself for quiet time in your own little corner of the world. The Lord will meet you in your sanctuary. Just name the time and place. Prepare yourself by leaving behind agendas, schedules, and to-do lists. Deliberately let go of your cares and relax your body and mind. Then fill yourself with God's presence and discover more about yourself and the one who loves you. Allow God to restore you to wholeness, give you a new perspective, refresh your mind, give you the fuel to move through whatever tomorrow may bring.

There is time in which to be, simply to be, that time in which God quietly tells us who we are and who he wants us to be. It is then that God can take our emptiness and fill it up with what he wants, and drain away the business with which we inevitably get involved in the dailyness of human living.

—MADELEINE L'ENGLE

God said to Moses: "My presence shall go with you, and I will give you rest."

Exodus 33:14 NASB

A Moment to Refresh

How priceless is your unfailing love! Both high and low among men find refuge in the shadow of your wings.

Psalm 36:7

I have stilled and quieted my soul; like a weaned child with its mother, like a weaned child is my soul within me.

Psalm 131:2

The fruit of righteousness will be peace; the effect of righteousness will be quietness and confidence forever.

Isaiah 32:17

The LORD makes me lie down in green pastures, he leads me beside quiet waters, he restores my soul.

Psalm 23:2–3

If you have an important decision to make or you find yourself in circumstances where you do not know what is best to do or answer, spend at least one night in meditation. You will not be sorry.

—AMISH PROVERB

My people will live in peaceful dwelling places, in secure homes, in undisturbed places of rest.

Isaiah 32:18

Let me see you in the sanctuary; let me see how mighty and glorious you are.

Psalm 63:2 GNT

O God, You are awesome from Your sanctuary. The God of Israel Himself gives strength and power to the people. Blessed be God!

Psalm 68:35 NASB

Find rest, O my soul, in God alone; my hope comes from him.

Psalm 62:5

Loneliness is inner emptiness. Solitude is inner fulfillment. Solitude is a state of mind and heart.

—RICHARD FOSTER

Reserved for You

A Moment to Pause

Isn't it amazing that you came prepackaged in your individual personality? You have unique gifts and abilities. Maybe you are a whiz at organizing or enjoy working with details that would frustrate others. Maybe you are a people person and a natural leader.

In ancient times, talents were actually a form of money, but in Jesus' parable of the talents they represent the inborn resources given by God. The story begins with an estate master, about to leave on a journey, who entrusts his money to his servants "each according to his ability." Each servant was expected to manage wisely what he had received. When the master returned a year later, he was pleased to find that two servants had made good investments and doubled the money. But the third one trembled to confess, "I was afraid and hid your talent in the ground."

What are your gifts and abilities? Are you good with your hands? Do you have a knack for decorating? Do you have a good singing voice? In your quiet time, ask God to show you how to multiply your talents so that you can serve God and others.

Our gifts are from God arranged by infinite wisdom, notes that make up the scores of creation's loftiest symphony, threads that compose the master tapestry of the universe.

—A. W. Tozer

A Moment to Reflect

God has arranged a special role for you to play in this life. He's reserved an adventure mapped out just for you, a trip to a destiny only you can fulfill. This role requires your specific talents, your inborn personality, and all your experiences, the bad as well as the good.

As you long to have your heart right with the Lord, you'll be eager to serve him with what he's graciously given you. As you draw close to the Lord, be aware of the passions that motivate you. See how they are partnered with your gifts and abilities. Allow God to propel you into your purpose, and experience joy as you invest your talents for him.

He designed our lives for work and pleasure,
We were created by God, as finest treasure.
His precious gifts are so worldly, yet divine,
If we choose to use them to bless mankind.

He has granted everyone the divine ability,
To be a brilliant light through our creativity.
So wisely invest all gifts that God has given,
For your great reward, here and in Heaven.

—Sylvia Lavallée

You have been faithful with a few things; I will put you in charge of many things. Come and share your master's happiness!

Matthew 25:21

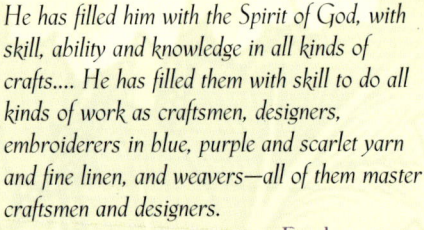

A Moment to Refresh

He has filled him with the Spirit of God, with skill, ability and knowledge in all kinds of crafts.... He has filled them with skill to do all kinds of work as craftsmen, designers, embroiderers in blue, purple and scarlet yarn and fine linen, and weavers—all of them master craftsmen and designers.

Exodus 35:31, 35

There are different kinds of gifts, but the same Spirit. There are different kinds of service, but the same Lord. There are different kinds of working, but the same God works all of them in all men.

1 Corinthians 12:4–6

Each one has a special gift from God, one person this gift, another one that gift.

1 Corinthians 7:7 GNT

To be granted some kind of usable talent and to be able to use it to the fullest extent of which you are capable—this to me, is a kind of joy that is almost unequaled.

—Lawrence Welk

Each one should use whatever gift he has received to serve others, faithfully administering God's grace in its various forms. If anyone speaks, he should do it as one speaking the very words of God. If anyone serves, he should do it with the strength God provides, so that in all things God may be praised through Jesus Christ.
1 Peter 4:10–11

God's gifts and his call are irrevocable.
Romans 11:29

We are to use our different gifts in accordance with the grace that God has given us.
Romans 12:6 GNT

God's gifts put man's best dreams to shame.

—Elizabeth Barrett Browning

Feminine Magic

A Moment to Pause

The Victorian woman of the 1800s had gracious manners and went to great lengths to remain feminine. Her tightly drawn corset ensured a shapely waist for satin gowns with balloon sleeves and billowing, hoop skirts. An elegant hostess, she was often called the "angel in the house." Tea was served in her finest bone china on a lace-covered table. Proper ladies would not be so immodest, of course, to discuss certain private matters. Women were not expected to have strong opinions, and they were not encouraged to explore opportunities outside the home.

Things have changed. Many women today dress in jeans or casual skirts or pants around the house and drink from mugs with favorite slogans. And women aren't quite so shy about speaking candidly. Nevertheless, femininity should not be neglected.

What makes you feel feminine? Is it wearing soft colors, a special perfume, a delicate piece of jewelry? Maybe you love having roses on the table or sipping an exotic tea from a china cup and saucer. Incorporate something delicate into your life this week. Experiment. Express your femininity in your own personal way.

A thing of beauty is a joy forever;
Its loveliness increases; it will never
Pass into nothingness.
—John Keats

A Moment to Reflect

God rejoices in the magic of your womanhood. The Bible celebrates feminine beauty. Tuck this truth in your heart—the Lord sees you as a "garden fountain, a well of flowing water" (Song of Solomon 4:15). God rejoices in the magnificence of your womanhood, and he gave it to you as a gift to be cultivated.

As you connect with the gift of your femininity, enjoy the deeper satisfaction of feeling at home in your skin. Delight in God's company as you nurture the woman he's made you to be.

As The Holy Master Potter,
With His love, so patiently,
Unfolds my spirit like a rose,
He reveals the beauty in me.

....

His vessel of pure loveliness,
Now shines in brilliant light,
A woman of great worth,
In whom, God can delight.

—Sylvia Lavallée

All beautiful you are, my darling; there is no flaw in you.

Song of Solomon 4:7

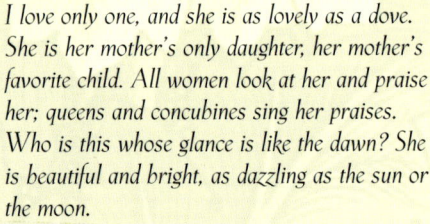

A Moment to Refresh

I love only one, and she is as lovely as a dove. She is her mother's only daughter, her mother's favorite child. All women look at her and praise her; queens and concubines sing her praises. Who is this whose glance is like the dawn? She is beautiful and bright, as dazzling as the sun or the moon.

Song of Songs 6:9–10 GNT

Your beauty should be that of your inner self, the unfading beauty of a gentle and quiet spirit, which is of great worth in God's sight. For this is the way the holy women of the past who put their hope in God used to make themselves beautiful.

1 Peter 3:4–5

He hath made his wonderful works to be remembered: the LORD is gracious and full of compassion.

Psalm 111:4 KJV

True strength is delicate.

—Louise Nevelson

When men began to increase in number on the earth and daughters were born to them, the sons of God saw that the daughters of men were beautiful.
Genesis 6:1–2

Paul wrote: I also want women to dress modestly, with decency and propriety, not the braided hair or gold or pearls or expensive clothes, but with good deeds.
1 Timothy 2:9–10

O my dove, in the clefts of the rock, in the secret place of the steep pathway, let me see your form, let me hear your voice, for your voice is sweet, and your form is lovely.
Song of Solomon 2:14 NASB

Thy lips are like a thread of scarlet, and thy speech is comely.
Song of Solomon 4:3 KJV

Honor women! They entwine and weave heavenly roses in our earthly life.

—Johan Christoph von Schiller

Renew an Old Friendship

A Moment to Pause

Friends come and go, but some share special pieces of your past and warm up your world. Gail discovered this at her first class reunion when she saw her old gang, the true-blue friends who were more like sisters than her own. They had yelled cheers at football games, strung crepe paper through the gym for proms, and huddled in sleeping bags under the stars, giggling over boys.

Catching up on each other's life, they celebrated each other's marriage, babies, and dreams come true. And they cried—over divorce, struggles, and disappointment. But when the night was over, they knew one thing. They didn't want to let their friendship slip away again. So now, once a year, they rent a cabin for a long weekend, frolic like carefree teenagers, and share their deepest thoughts, hopes and fears. They may not solve any problems, but they bolster each other up and leave refreshed.

Do you have an old friend from way back when? When you dared to be yourself, when you felt accepted and loved? Find out where she is now, and then call or write her. Tell her how much she means to you, how you cherish the memories the two of you share. Set a date to get together with her, and then do it.

Friends in your life are like pillars on your porch. Sometimes they hold you up, and sometimes they lean on you. Sometimes it's just enough to know they're standing by.
—Author Unknown

A Moment to Reflect

It has been said that a faithful friend is an image of God, that a faithful friend is someone who understands who you are, where you've been, everything you've gone through. A faithful friend is someone who believes in you and accepts you exactly the way you are, someone who speaks the painful truth with loving words, someone with whom you feel safe, someone who offers a warm hug when you face disappointment and a hearty applause with every success.

God will wrap his arms around you through the arms of a good friend. He'll remind you through her that he can always be reached, that he longs to be your familiar and trusted companion who desires a daily reunion with you.

*We all need God's mercy,
We all need God's love.
We all need forgiveness
And grace from above.
We all need redemption,
We all need a Friend.
We all need a Savior
To have peace within.*

—Jan McIntosh

You understand, O LORD, remember me and care for me.

Jeremiah 15:15

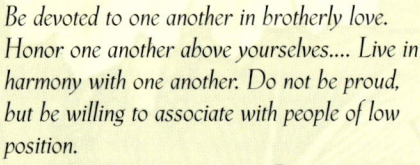

A Moment to Refresh

Be devoted to one another in brotherly love. Honor one another above yourselves.... Live in harmony with one another. Do not be proud, but be willing to associate with people of low position.

Romans 12:10, 16

How good and how pleasant it is for brethren to dwell together in unity!

Psalm 133:1 KJV

I always thank God for you because of his grace given you in Christ Jesus.

1 Corinthians 1:4

Perfume and incense bring joy to the heart, and the pleasantness of one's friend springs from his earnest counsel.

Proverbs 27:9

The fingers of God touch your life when you touch a friend.

—MARY DAWN HUGHES

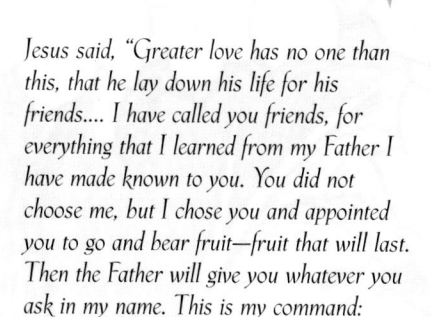

Jesus said, "Greater love has no one than this, that he lay down his life for his friends.... I have called you friends, for everything that I learned from my Father I have made known to you. You did not choose me, but I chose you and appointed you to go and bear fruit—fruit that will last. Then the Father will give you whatever you ask in my name. This is my command: Love each other."

John 15:13, 15–17

Let us love one another, for love comes from God. Everyone who loves has been born of God and loves God.

1 John 4:7

Jesus said, "Where two or three come together in my name, there am I with them."

Matthew 18:20

Girlfriends are forever friends when they're bound together with the love of God.

—JANET HOLM MCHENRY

The Boomerang of Love

A Moment to Pause

When you think of a boomerang, what comes to mind? Probably a bent or curved stick that you throw high in the air. It eventually swings around and comes right back to the thrower's hand. Children often wonder if the amazing stick is magic. Invented by the Australian Aborigines, the boomerang is actually the first man-made flying machine, an amazing hunk of wood that works on complex principles of physics. If you want it to come back to you, there are certain techniques that must be mastered. It is certainly one of the most remarkable tools in history.

You are familiar with the saying, Love isn't love until you give it away. Like the boomerang, love is an action, an activity. Love is not something we feel; rather, love is something we do. It's easy to master, and the how-to manual is easy to follow. Just throw love away, high and wide. Give it out as much and as often as you can.

Consider ways you can give away love this week. Take a meal to someone who's ill. Write a note of encouragement and include a little cash for someone in need. Baby-sit for a single mom in your church. Give love freely and watch it return to you from unexpected places.

Love is like the five loaves and two fishes. It doesn't start to multiply until you give it away.
—Author Unknown

A Moment to Reflect

When one loves God, it is natural to pass on that love to others, for love is the essence of God. When one is filled to the brim with the affirming love of the heavenly Father, love springs forth. When you cast forth love to others, you embody the commandment to love one another as Christ loved you. As you give yourself with joy to others, others will see the Lord, and his love circles back to replenish you. It may be as a warm note from a special friend or a smile from a stranger, but however it comes you'll be lifted higher than you can imagine.

You can smell it in a flower,
You can see it in the sky,
You can feel it soft and gentle
As a summer breeze blows by—
The touch of love is in the air!
You can show it with a smile,
You will know it when you pray,
It's a gift that's all around you
And inside you every day—
God's touch of love is everywhere!

—ALICE JOYCE DAVIDSON

No one has seen God at any time; if we love one another, God abides in us, and His love is perfected in us.

1 John 4:12 NASB

A Moment to Refresh

Jesus said, "I give you a new commandment: love one another. As I have loved you, so you must love one another. If you have love for one another, then everyone will know that you are my disciples."

John 13:34–35 GNT

Mercy, peace and love be yours in abundance.

Jude 2

The LORD is righteous in all his ways and loving toward all he has made.

Psalm 145:17

Love always protects, always trusts, always hopes, always perseveres.

1 Corinthians 13:8

Love is the only force capable of transforming an enemy into a friend.

—Martin Luther King

We love because he first loved us....
Whoever loves God must also love his brother.

1 John 4:19, 21

Since you are God's dear children, you must try to be like him. Your life must be controlled by love, just as Christ loved us and gave his life for us as a sweet-smelling offering and sacrifice that pleases God.

Ephesians 5:1–2 GNT

Having loved his own who were in the world, Jesus now showed them the full extent of his love.

John 13:1

Love cures people—both the ones who give it and the ones who receive it.

—Karl Augustus Menninger

Through a Child's Eyes

A Moment to Pause

Back in the 1930s her dimpled, smiling face was a joyous tonic for people caught in an economic crisis, people who were losing their jobs and struggling to put food on the table. In movies like Little Miss Marker, Bright Eyes, and Stand Up and Cheer, Shirley Temple charmed her way into viewers' hearts. The infectious optimism of a child made people forget their troubles.

The eagerness to venture beyond boundaries toward possibilities can be seen in a child's sparkling eyes. Now think back to the time when you were young and eager to explore the world through endless play.

When was the last time you climbed into a swing at the park and let yourself glide higher and higher until you were wondrously dizzy? When was the last time you skipped along? When was the last time you tried to win a footrace? Experience again the delight of a child's-eye view, and see the world and all its fresh and new possibilities.

From her first breath, she captivates us and commands our attention. As she discovers the many wonders of life, her eager spirit and fresh perspective inspire us to appreciate the world anew through her eyes.
—Arlene Benedict

A Moment to Reflect

As a little girl, you were innocent and always hopeful, filled with simple faith. All you needed was a loving look and a gentle touch to feel secure and content. You knew faith and trust, which are second nature to a child.

Jesus said that everyone should have a childlike faith. Pray for that right now. Know that God will shelter you and provide all your needs. Your faith can be a wide-eyed, innocent faith that accepts and waits, a faith without question marks, a faith that accepts that understanding will come later.

To be a child.... It is to believe in love, to believe in loveliness, to believe in belief; it is to be so little that the elves can reach to whisper in your ear; it is to turn pumpkins into coaches, and mice into horses, lowness into loftiness and nothing into everything, for each child has its fairy godmother in its soul.

—Francis Thompson Shelly

Jesus said, "Everything is possible for him who believes."

Mark 9:23

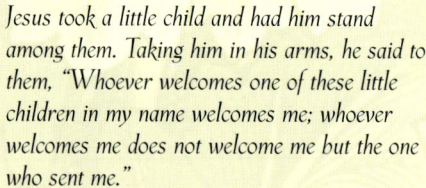

A Moment to Refresh

Jesus took a little child and had him stand among them. Taking him in his arms, he said to them, "Whoever welcomes one of these little children in my name welcomes me; whoever welcomes me does not welcome me but the one who sent me."

Mark 9:36–37

Then some children were brought to Him so that He might lay His hands on them and pray; and the disciples rebuked them. But Jesus said, "Let the children alone, and do not hinder them from coming to Me; for the kingdom of heaven belongs to such as these."

Matthew 19:13–14 NASB

Jesus said, "Whoever humbles himself like this child is the greatest in the kingdom of heaven."

Matthew 18:4

Children have neither past nor future; and that which seldom happens to us, they rejoice in the present.

—JEAN DE LA BRUYERE

Blessed are the pure in heart, for they shall see God.... Rejoice and be glad, because great is your reward in heaven.
Matthew 5:8, 12

We walk by faith, not by sight.
2 Corinthians 5:7 NASB

The goal of this command is love, which comes from a pure heart and a good conscience and a sincere faith.
1 Timothy 1:5

The LORD guides the humble in what is right and teaches them his way.... May integrity and uprightness protect me, because my hope is in you.
Psalm 25:9, 21

Children are God's apostles, day by day Sent forth to preach of love, and hope, and peace.

—JAMES RUSSELL LOWELL

Crowd Out Worry

A Moment to Pause

Worry can be a big problem. It's not uncommon to worry when confronted with a problem. Or to take cares to bed and then wake up with a weight on one's mind. Because women are designed to nurture and protect others, it's hard to see loved ones struggle. Some women seem to slide naturally into thinking, *What if?*

Post this helpful hint for worry on your refrigerator:
KNEAD TODAY'S BREAD ONLY—TODAY'S BREAD
IS THE ONLY BREAD I CAN POSSIBLY EAT.
And pray:
*I know the things I worry about usually
never happen, Lord. Help me focus on today.
Tomorrow will take care of itself.*

When you find yourself loaded down with negative possibilities, crowd them out. Grab those worrisome thoughts, secure them with a big knot, and toss them up to God. Write your worries in the sand on the beach and watch the tide sweep them away. Mentally stuff them into a burlap sack and watch them round the bend in the river—they'll not return, because they can't float back upstream on their own.

*If only we could stop lamenting and look up. God is here.
Christ is risen. The Spirit has been poured out from on
high. All this we know as theological truth. It remains for
us to turn it into joyous spiritual experience.*
—A. W. Tozer

A Moment to Reflect

There is a difference between planning and worrying. One is time well spent, the other is time wasted. Worry never changes a thing except the worrier.

When you crowd out worry, you send anxiety packing. You travel lighter knowing you won't sink under today's load. It's only when tomorrow's cares are added to those of today that the weight is more than you can bear. God never intended you to worry, to fret over things beyond your control. When you concentrate on God's promises to meet all your needs, you fend off tensions of this world. God will replace your cares with a secret strength to endure what happens today, and release thoughts of all the things that might go wrong tomorrow.

*In prayerful moments
subtle peace comes
when I choose to drop
my fearful baggage
into Greater Arms.*

—CHARLOTTE ADELSPERGER

Jesus said, "How can any of you by worrying add a single hour to your span of life?"
Luke 12:25 NRSV

A Moment to Refresh

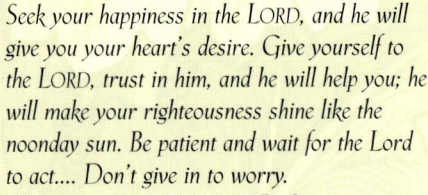

Seek your happiness in the LORD, and he will give you your heart's desire. Give yourself to the LORD, trust in him, and he will help you; he will make your righteousness shine like the noonday sun. Be patient and wait for the Lord to act.... Don't give in to worry.
Psalm 37:3–8 GNT

Make up your mind not to worry beforehand how you will defend yourselves. For I will give you words and wisdom that none of your adversaries will be able to resist or contradict.
Luke 21:14–15

"Peace I leave with you; my peace I give to you. I do not give as the world gives. Do not let your hearts be troubled and do not be afraid."
John 14:27

Worry gives a small thing a big shadow.

—Swedish Proverb

Jesus said, "I have told you these things, so that in me you may have peace. In this world you will have trouble. But take heart! I have overcome the world."

John 16:33

Cast your cares on the LORD and he will sustain you; he will never let the righteous fall.

Psalm 55:22

Jesus said, "Do not worry about your life, what you will eat or drink; or about your body, what you will wear. Is not life more important than food, and the body more important than clothes? Look at the birds of the air, they do not sow or reap or store away in barns, and yet your heavenly Father feeds them.... Do not worry about tomorrow, for tomorrow will worry about itself."

Matthew 6:25–26, 34

When worry is present, trust cannot crowd its way in.

—Billy Graham

Beauty in the Ordinary

A Moment to Pause

The world is impatient and fast changing, and progress is relentless. Technology is advancing at lightning speed. Nothing stays ordinary for long, so take a look around you now.

Lean back on your personal observation deck and view the commonplace in your life. Notice the run-of-the mill things in your world, those plain, everyday occurrences that are so easy to neglect.

Peek up at fleecy clouds that scurry across the sky like a bit of lace. Examine the folded bud of a flower waiting to burst forth in romantic color. Revel in the dawning wonder of a baby's face and the laughter of the children as they board the school bus. See the kindness in a loved one's eyes, the grit on the face of a mountain biker straining to make the hill. Enjoy the smell of a good cup of coffee brewing, the sound of a familiar Hi when you answer the phone.

See the beauty in the ordinary. Slow down and breathe the fragrance of the ordinary, the everyday things that sit along life's way. Remind yourself often to stop and smell the flowers.

I find each day too short for all the thoughts I want to think, all the walks I want to take, all the books I want to read, and all the friends I want to see. The longer I live the more my mind dwells on the beauty and the wonder of the world.
—John Burroughs

A Moment to Reflect

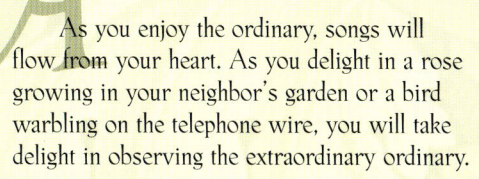

As you enjoy the ordinary, songs will flow from your heart. As you delight in a rose growing in your neighbor's garden or a bird warbling on the telephone wire, you will take delight in observing the extraordinary ordinary.

God reveals his presence in the familiar—the leafy trees, the shadows cast, the trampled path. God reveals his presence in the beat of your heart and the breath you take. You have access to God's presence anywhere, anytime. The more you delight in the backdrop of the routine, you will discover yourself more satisfied, more grateful and more in touch with the Lord.

God can paint rich hues
on the misty memories of my past.
He can shine a guiding ray
on my choices for the future.
But God's love reigns best
when he, in nearness, holds
this very moment in his hand.

—CHARLOTTE ADELSPERGER

One thing I ask of the LORD, this is what I seek: that I may dwell in the house of the LORD all the days of my life, to gaze upon the beauty of the LORD.

Psalm 27:4

A Moment to Refresh

He has made everything beautiful in its time. He has also set eternity in the hearts of men; yet they cannot fathom what God has done from beginning to end.

Ecclesiastes 3:11

How beautiful on the mountains are the feet of those who bring good news, who proclaim peace, who bring good tidings, who proclaim salvation, who say to Zion, "Your God reins!"

Isaiah 52:7

Great are the works of the LORD; they are pondered by all who delight in him. Glorious and majestic are his deeds and his righteousness endures forever.

Psalm 111:2–3

Unwrap the hidden beauties in an ordinary day.

—GERHARD E. FROST

O LORD, our Sovereign, how majestic is your name in all the earth! You have set your glory above the heavens.

Psalm 8:1 NRSV

Let us acknowledge the LORD; let us press on to acknowledge him. As surely as the sun rises, he will appear; he will come to us like the winter rains, like the spring rains that water the earth.

Hosea 6:3

When [the people] saw the courage of Peter and John and realized that they were unschooled, ordinary men, they were astonished and they took note that these men had been with Jesus.

Acts 4:13

The best things are nearest; breath in your nostrils, light in your eyes, flowers at your feet, duties at your hand, the path of God just before you.

—ROBERT LOUIS STEVENSON

A Grateful Heart

A Moment to Pause

Sometimes things go wrong all day—your computer freezes up during an important project, you get a flat tire when you're running late, the washing machine snaps a belt when it's full of soggy towels. It is easy to lose perspective at times like these. It is easy to see more rain than rainbow.

But take a moment to think of something you can give thanks for. Maybe it's a dear friend who sent you a card. Perhaps it's the helpful stranger who picked up the money you unknowingly dropped in the grocery line. Maybe it's the coupon you clipped out of the paper for a discount on an oil change.

Count everything you can be thankful for today. Remind yourself you have been given an abundance of blessings that enrich, brighten, and sweeten your life. All around you are little blessings. Point them out to yourself and watch them multiply. The more you give thanks, the more reasons you'll find to be thankful.

Then tell others how thankful you are. Try thanking the store clerk for her efficiency, the bus driver for getting you there safely, the gardener for making your neighbor's lawn look so nice. See how many hearts you can lift and smiles you can elicit.

Every day, see how many things you can be thankful for. Say them over to yourself. Face the difficulties. They have to be dealt with. But, a positive, thankful psychology has written in it the power to make things good, better, best.

—Norman Vincent Peale

A Moment to Reflect

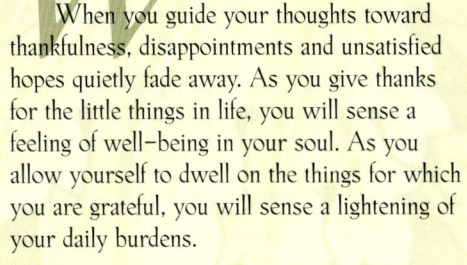

When you guide your thoughts toward thankfulness, disappointments and unsatisfied hopes quietly fade away. As you give thanks for the little things in life, you will sense a feeling of well-being in your soul. As you allow yourself to dwell on the things for which you are grateful, you will sense a lightening of your daily burdens.

Direct your mind toward God's goodness and the many unexpected surprises that await you. Be assured that he is in control. Troubles no longer will seem insurmountable; problems no longer will loom so large.

I give thanks, O God, for all
You have so lovingly done for me!
For each need comes Your faithfulness.
During suffering comes Your compassion.
On every journey comes Your closeness.
My deepest praise sings out
in a blended anthem with believers
all over the world—thanking You for
the abundant life found in Christ Jesus!

—CHARLOTTE ADELSPERGER

Give thanks to the LORD, call on his name; make known among the nations what he has done. Sing to him, sing praise to him; tell of all his wonderful acts.

1 Chronicles 16:8–9

A Moment to Refresh

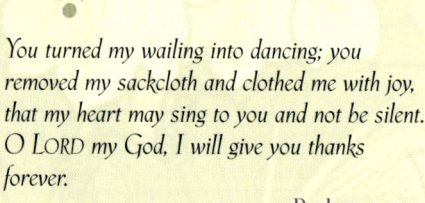

You turned my wailing into dancing; you removed my sackcloth and clothed me with joy, that my heart may sing to you and not be silent. O LORD my God, I will give you thanks forever.

Psalm 30:11–12

Enter his gates with thanksgiving and his courts with praise; give thanks to him and praise his name. For the LORD is good and his love endures forever; his faithfulness continues through all generations.

Psalm 100:4–5

Let them give thanks to the LORD for his unfailing love and his wonderful deeds for men, for he satisfied the thirsty and fills the hungry with good things.

Psalm 107:8–9

Cultivate a thankful spirit! It will be to you a perpetual feast.

—JOHN R. MACDUFF

I have set the LORD always before me. Because he is at my right side, I will not be shaken. Therefore my heart is glad and my tongue rejoices.... You have made known to me the path of life; you will fill me with joy in your presence, with eternal pleasures at your right hand.
Psalm 16:8–9, 11

Everything God created is good, and nothing is to be rejected if it is received with thanksgiving, because it is consecrated by the word of God and prayer.
1 Timothy 4:4–5

Live in Christ, rooted and built up in him, strengthened in the faith as you were taught, and overflowing with thankfulness.
Colossians 2:6–7

Let us give thanks for Someone to thank.

—GERHARD E. FROST

Chuckle a Day

A Moment to Pause

Do you laugh regularly? Laughter decreases the mood-altering hormones that play havoc with your attitude, stirs the blood, expands the chest, clears out the brain. Laughter reduces stress and makes you feel better.

Laughter, from a gentle chuckle to a hearty giggle, is tonic for the soul. It is a shock absorber that eases the blows of life. Laughter doesn't erase the problem, but it can sure make things more pleasant for a while.

Resolve to incorporate humor into your life. Create a humor first-aid kit, your own survival gear for stressful times. Fill it with things that tickle your funny bone—sidesplitting jokes, clever stories, witty greeting cards, funny cartoons, crazy hats, old photos that will crack a smile. Schedule a time each week to get out your kit and spend time laughing.

Humor is contagious. Make sure to pass it on. Call a friend and share one of your favorite jokes or read a whimsical story. Send an amusing card to someone who needs a good hearty chuckle today.

Mirth is God's medicine. Everybody ought to bathe in it. Grim care, moroseness, anxiety—all this rust of life ought to be scoured off by the oil of mirth.
—Henry Ward Beecher

A Moment to Reflect

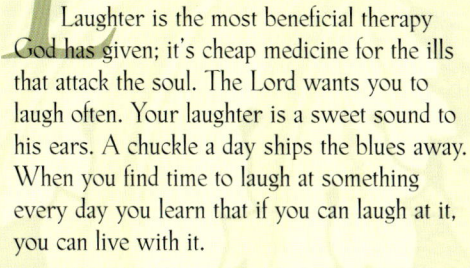

Laughter is the most beneficial therapy God has given; it's cheap medicine for the ills that attack the soul. The Lord wants you to laugh often. Your laughter is a sweet sound to his ears. A chuckle a day ships the blues away. When you find time to laugh at something every day you learn that if you can laugh at it, you can live with it.

Martin Luther said, "If you're not allowed to laugh in heaven, I don't want to go there." Certainly, laughter will be magnified in heaven, but it's yours here and now, so indulge often. Joy, creativity, fun—these are God's creations, fringe benefits of the Spirit-filled life.

You and I were created for joy, and if we miss it, we miss the reason for our existence.... If our joy is honest joy, it must somehow be congruous with human tragedy. This is the test of joy's integrity; is it compatible with pain. Only the heart that hurts has a right to joy.

—Lewis B. Smedes

Sarah said, "God has brought me laughter, and everyone who hears about this will laugh with me."

Genesis 21:6

A Moment to Refresh

She is clothed with strength and dignity; she can laugh at the days to come.

Proverbs 31:25

A glad heart makes a cheerful countenance, but by sorrow of heart the spirit is broken.

Proverbs 15:13 NRSV

A cheerful look brings joy to the heart, and good news gives health to the bones.

Proverbs 15:30

May the righteous be glad and rejoice before God; may they be happy and joyful.

Psalm 68:3

A good laugh heals a lot of hurts.

—MADELEINE L'ENGLE

He will fill your mouth with laughter and your lips with shouts of joy.

Job 8:21

My soul will rejoice in the Lord and delight in his salvation.

Psalm 35:9

Is anyone among you in trouble? He should pray. Is anyone happy? Let him sing songs of praise.

James 5:13

Let all who take refuge in you be glad; let them ever sing for joy.

Psalm 5:11

Laughter is a tranquilizer with no side effects.

—ARNOLD GLASCOW

Just Enough

A Moment to Pause

When Moses and the Israelites were trapped at the Red Sea, God brought them miraculously through. Yet two months later, the Israelites were weary and tired of eating the same old food. They complained, "Why can't we be back in Egypt?" Did they truly want captivity again? No. They had simply forgotten God's faithfulness and felt pressured. In their frustration, they missed the lesson: contentment is not the fulfillment of what one has; it is the realization of how much one already has.

Many people view happiness as a future state, something to achieve later, when a certain goal is reached. Have you ever reached that goal only to find the happiness short-lived? Have you ever reached that goal only to find yourself already looking to something else for fulfillment?

Think about all the things you love about your life. Jot down a list of everything you already have. Ignore what might be or how you wish things could be in an ideal world, and cultivate an appreciation for life just as it is. Contentment is sweet to your soul.

The children of Israel did not find in the manna all the sweetness and strength they might have found in it; not because the manna didn't contain them, but because they longed for other meat.
—*Saint John of the Cross*

A Moment to Reflect

Paul reminded the Philippians to be content with what they had. He also urged them to understand that there is a difference between what they may want and what they needed. That is God's desire for you as well.

God will supply your every need, whether physical or emotional, whether nourishment for the body or for the soul. By trusting God completely, your attitudes and desires become his. Your priorities will change. You will feel full and satisfied with what he provides, no matter what happens.

O what a happy soul am I!
Although I cannot see,
I am resolved that in this world
Contented I will be;
How many blessings I enjoy
That other people don't!
To weep and sigh because I'm blind,
I cannot, and I won't.

—FANNY CROSBY

I am not saying this because I am in need, for I have learned to be content whatever the circumstances.

Philippians 4:11

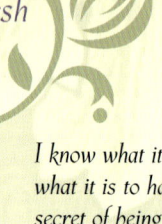

A Moment to Refresh

I know what it is to be in need, and I know what it is to have plenty. I have learned the secret of being content in any and every situation, whether well fed or hungry, whether living in plenty or in want. I can do all things through Christ who gives me strength.

Philippians 4:12–13

The fear of the LORD leads to life: Then one rests content, untouched by trouble.

Proverbs 19:23

Put your hope in the LORD both now and forevermore.

Psalm 131:3

You are my God my savior, and my hope is in you all day long.

Psalm 25:5

When life isn't the way you like, like it the way it is.

—JEWISH PROVERB

Godliness with contentment is great gain. For we brought nothing into the world, and we can take nothing out of it. But if we have food and clothing, we will be content with that.

1 Timothy 6:6–8

Keep your lives free from the love of money, and be content with what you have, for he has said, "Never will I leave you; never will I forsake you." So we can say with confidence, "The Lord is my helper; I will not be afraid. What can anyone do to me?"

Hebrews 13:5–6

When times are good, be happy; and when times are bad, consider: God has made the one as well as the other. Therefore, a man cannot discover anything about his future.

Ecclesiastes 7:14

Sweet are the thoughts that savor content; The quiet mind is richer than a crown.

—ROBERT GREENE

Roll with the Flow

A Moment to Pause

Let go and let God. How many times have you heard that? It sounds like a simple solution, but how does one achieve it? Do you find yourself instead paddling upstream, struggling against the current, pushing yourself onward? Do you get a few scrapes in the process?

Contentment requires flexibility, a willingness to bend. Are you resisting something right now? Stand up, take a deep breath, hold it for a few seconds, and then exhale slowly. Bend at the waist and let your arms hang loose. Part company with your tension. Feel it float away.

Remind yourself often that it's easier to bend than to break. There are some things you simply can't control. You may be at the wheel of the ship, but the rudder is broken and you can't steer it right now. You have no choice but to sit back, let go, and trust. God knows the situation, he knows exactly where you are. Be willing to glide along, to roll with the flow, to end up in a different place on the map than you'd first planned.

Teach me to do your will,
for you are my God;
may your good Spirit
lead me on level ground.
For your name's sake, O Lord, preserve my life;
in your righteousness bring me out of trouble.
—Psalm 143:10–11

A Moment to Reflect

The more you yield, the more you become a woman who can be molded like clay in the hand of the potter, your God. He cannot work with clay that is dry or rigid, and he longs to fashion and shape you for his glory, and your best.

Though it's hard to understand everything that happens, practice yielding to whatever life brings. Trust that God is at the wheel and give him the control. When you are more flexible, you'll be more resilient to the storms, you can bounce right back from disappointments. Your heart will be limber and ready and prepared to accept what comes.

*Every day our Lord invites me along
to discover for myself the
sparkling dew of his forgiveness,
inner warmth of his love,
embracing breeze of his spirit.
....
Oh, how I want to yield
to my God in our love journey,
side by side.*

—CHARLOTTE ADELSPERGER

The LORD will fulfill his purpose for me; your love O LORD endures forever—do not abandon the work of your hands

Psalm 138:8

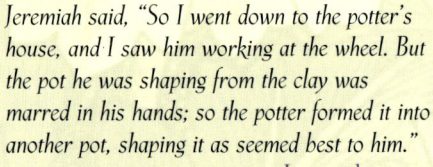

A Moment to Refresh

Jeremiah said, "So I went down to the potter's house, and I saw him working at the wheel. But the pot he was shaping from the clay was marred in his hands; so the potter formed it into another pot, shaping it as seemed best to him."

Jeremiah 18:3–4

The nations will see your righteousness, and all the kings your glory; you will be called by a new name that the mouth of the LORD will bestow. You will be a crown of splendor in the LORD's hand, a royal diadem in the hand of your God.

Isaiah 62:2–3

It is God who works in you to will and to act according to his good purpose.

Philippians 2:13

Lead on, O King eternal: we follow, not with fears; for gladness breaks like morning where'er thy face appears.

—Ernest Warburton Shurtleff

If you indeed cry out for insight, and raise your voice for understanding; if you seek it like silver, and search for it as for hidden treasures—then you will understand the fear of the LORD and find the knowledge of God. For the LORD gives wisdom; from his mouth come knowledge and understanding.
Proverbs 2:3–6 NRSV

I will guide you in the way of wisdom and lead you along straight paths. When you walk, your steps will not be hampered; when you run, you will not stumble.
Proverbs 4:11–12

You are my rock and my fortress, for the sake of your name lead and guide me.
Psalm 31:3

I never really look for anything. What God throws my way comes. I wake up in the morning and whichever way God turns my feet, I go.

—Pearl Bailey

Heaven's Stairs

A Moment to Pause

Do you need comfort, reassurance, or guidance right now? Retreat to your quiet spot and steep yourself in prayer. You don't have to be eloquent, just sincere. Come to him just as you are. Jesus said that "the kingdom of God is within you."

Close your mind to everything around you and open the eyes of your soul. Start by praying the Lord's Prayer. Pour out your heart to him as a sweet innocent child. Between each verse, pause for a while. Feel deep within your spirit the holy presence of the Lord.

As you speak the prayer, bring all your needs before him. Be candid; you can lay all your concerns before God; he will understand all your desires, yearnings, and feelings. God does not tire of hearing the sound of your heart expressing its deepest feelings.

Then give God a gift; tell him he may work in your heart as he chooses. His will, not yours. Don't try to imagine what he'll do or how he'll work out the details. Simply seek his presence, and let that be enough.

Real prayer is simply being in the presence of God.... I just want to be with him for a time, to feel his comradeship, his concert, his caring around me and about me, and then to go out to a world warmer because I spent an hour with him.
—*Robert A. Cook*

A Moment to Reflect

Prayer is the staircase to heaven, a climb that leads to the treasures of God's mercies and blessings. Your prayers link you to God and allow you to sense his presence and get to know him intimately.

When you speak honestly in your own personality, holding nothing back, God becomes your trusted friend. You love and enjoy him just because he is there with you. Pray with a believing heart, and your relationship with God will deepen and mature. Your spirit will be at peace. Praying souls are confident and peaceful.

When I feel still and very empty
I try to turn my thoughts to prayer,
A little light turns on inside
And suddenly My God is there.

My doubts come from their stony places,
He turns each one into a flower,
My heart gets into heaven's gate,
I'm linked again with Him in prayer.

—Marion Schoeberlein

Very early in the morning, while it was still dark, Jesus got up, left the house and went off to a solitary place, where he prayed.

Mark 1:35

A Moment to Refresh

Do not be anxious about anything, but in everything, by prayer and petition, with thanksgiving, present your requests to God. And the peace of God, which transcends all understanding, will guard your hearts and your minds in Christ Jesus.

Philippians 4:6–7

I call to God, and the LORD saves me. Evening, morning and noon I cry out in distress, and he hears my voice.

Psalm 55:16–17

God has surely listened and heard my voice in prayer. Praise be to God, who has not rejected my prayer or withheld his love from me!

Psalm 66:19–20

A prayer in its simplest definition is merely a wish turned Godward.

—Phillips Brooks

The LORD has heard my cry for mercy; the LORD accepts my prayer.

Psalm 6:9

I call upon you, O LORD; come quickly to me; give ear to my voice when I call you. Let my prayer be counted as incense before you, and the lifting up of my hands as an evening sacrifice.

Psalm 141:1–2 NRSV

Jesus said, "Therefore, I tell you, whatever you ask for in prayer, believe that you have received it, and it will be yours. And when you stand praying, if you hold anything against anyone, forgive him, so that your Father in heaven may forgive you your sins."

Mark 11:24–25

Prayer is like the turning of an electric switch. It does not create the current; it simply provides a channel through which the electric current may flow.

—Max Handel

It's a Wonderful Life

A Moment to Pause

Find a few hours this week to watch the video of It's a Wonderful Life. Pop some corn and settle in, but before you hit Play, reflect on this. A few typed pages written as a Christmas card in 1945, found its way to Frank Capra. The story takes place in a small town, where an average man feels that success passed him by. When disaster strikes, he wishes he'd never been born. Not a praying man, George Bailey begs God to show him the way. A guardian angel arrives and helps him see that he has everything truly valuable in life right before him. What an idea!

Acclaimed by critics and the public, the movie made little profit and was soon forgotten, until years later when it became a beloved family classic. Why? In a gushy sentimental way, It's a Wonderful Life mirrors our own doubts, loss of faith, and the mistaken wish, if only I was somebody else. As George wrestles with it all, Mary Bailey is gentle and supportive, but when things get desperate, she takes control and brings about the miracle they need.

Life doesn't always provide perfect happy endings, but we need this movie's message. Accept who you are, what you have been given, and the blessing you've been to others.

Let no one say we are worthless. God is not a foolish speculator; he would never invest in worthless property.
—Erwin W. Lutzer

A Moment to Reflect

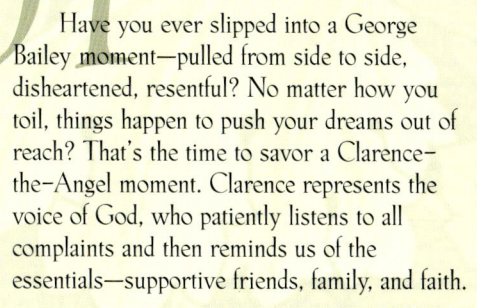

Have you ever slipped into a George Bailey moment—pulled from side to side, disheartened, resentful? No matter how you toil, things happen to push your dreams out of reach? That's the time to savor a Clarence-the-Angel moment. Clarence represents the voice of God, who patiently listens to all complaints and then reminds us of the essentials—supportive friends, family, and faith.

As you reflect on your life, know that God is always near, always approachable, always eager for you to know how irreplaceable you are. Your life has touched many others. You have a unique story written just for you.

*Feeling pushed and perplexed,
I want to escape—to find myself.
....
God knows my soul
and I can tell him all.
So I take a fresh path to travel with my Lord,
and find myself on a holy highway
full of wonder and newness and hope.*

—CHARLOTTE ADELSPERGER

This is what the LORD says: "Stand at the crossroads and look; ask for the ancient paths, ask where the good way is, and walk in it, and you will find rest for your souls."

Jeremiah 6:16

A Moment to Refresh

The LORD is righteous in all his ways and loving toward all he has made. The Lord is near to all who call on him, to all who call on him in truth.

Psalm 145:17–18

I know that there is nothing better for men than to be happy and do good while they live.

Ecclesiastes 3:12

Jesus said, "I am the vine; you are the branches. If a man remains in me and I in him, he will bear much fruit."

John 15:5

The wisdom that comes from heaven is first of all pure; then peace-loving, considerate, submissive, full of mercy and good fruit, impartial and sincere. Peacemakers who live in peace raise a harvest of righteousness.

James 3:17–18

God rarely allows a soul to see how great a blessing he is.

—OSWALD CHAMBERS

You are the light of the world. A city on a hill cannot be hidden. Neither do people light a lamp and put it under a bowl. Instead they put it on its stand, and it gives light to everyone in the house. In the same way, let your light shine before men, that they may see your good deeds and praise your Father in heaven.

Matthew 5:14–16

The fruit of the Spirit is love, joy, peace, patience, kindness, goodness, faithfulness, gentleness and self-control.

Galatians 5:22–23

Who is wise and understanding among you? Let him show it by his good life, by deeds in the humility that comes from wisdom.

James 3:13

Every life is a fairy tale, written by God's fingers.

—HANS CHRISTIAN ANDERSEN

Memory's Attic

A Moment to Pause

Imagine an attic with a tiny window that lets in just enough light for an afternoon of discovery. There is an old dresser that held all your baby things, sleepers, and sweaters, all folded neatly. Breathe deeply. Can you smell the sweet talcum powder? And over there in the corner, see the old trunk with tarnished metal corners and leather straps? Take a peek inside. It's full of old feathery hats, shiny high-heeled shoes, and glittery gowns. Can you think of yourself all dressed up, playing make-believe; hosting a tea party for your favorite dolls like a grand duchess?

As you enjoy this moment, try to remember a specific pleasure from your past. Perhaps it was the day you wobbled down the sidewalk on your first two-wheeler, or the day you went barefoot on the lawn, or the day you read your first love letter. Perhaps it was a graduation, a special Christmas, a long-awaited vacation.

Nothing soothes the soul like a cherished memory that takes you back to a precious time. Memories like these are only meant to be rest stops along the way, places to drink in the wonder of days gone by, not to wish them back, but to relish them as part of you—who you were and who you will become.

Memory is the cabinet of imagination, the treasury of reason, the registry of conscience, and the council chamber of thought.
—Saint Basil

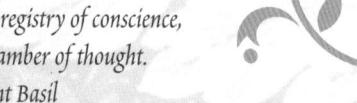

A Moment to Reflect

Sometimes the attic may seem a bit dark, the relics covered in soot, the ink long faded on the cherished letters. Still, God wants to explore with you. Go with him on a tour of the treasures in your heart. Take time to let him fill your mind with pleasant memories, the ones that will evoke pleasant feelings and fill you with nostalgia.

When God jogs your mind about the past, it won't be your regrets or the wounds you'd rather forget. He'll prompt you with warm thoughts that will affirm who you are and who you were meant to be, thoughts that refresh, renew and never fail to bring a smile.

God can paint rich hues on the misty memories of my past. He can shine a guiding ray on my choices for the future. But God's love reigns best when he, in nearness, holds this very moment in his hands.

—CHARLOTTE ADESLPERGER

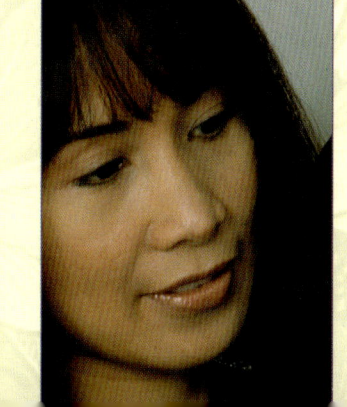

Whenever the rainbow appears in the clouds, I will see it and remember the everlasting covenant between God and all living creatures of every kind on earth.

Genesis 9:16

A Moment to Refresh

I remember the days of long ago; I meditate on all your works and consider what your hands have done. I spread out my hands to you; my soul thirsts for you like a parched land.

Psalm 143:5–6

So I will always remind you of these things, even though you know them and are firmly established in the truth you now have. I think it is right to refresh your memory as long as I live in the tent of this body, because I know that I will soon put it aside, as our Lord Jesus Christ has made clear to me.

2 Peter 1:12–14

I will remember the deeds of the LORD; yes, I will remember your miracles of long ago. I will meditate on all your works and consider all your mighty deeds.

Psalm 77:11–12

I have a room where into no one enters, save I myself alone. There sits a blessed memory on a throne. There, my life centers.

—CHRISTINA ROSSETTI

To him that is able to do immeasurably more than all we could ask or imagine, according to his power that is at work within us, to him be glory in the church and in Christ Jesus throughout all generations, forever and ever!

Ephesians 3:20–21

The LORD appeared to us in the past, saying: "I have loved you with an everlasting love; I have drawn you with loving-kindness. I will build you up again and you will be rebuilt."

Jeremiah 31:3–4

Sing to the LORD, all the earth; proclaim his salvation day after day. Declare his glory among the nations, his marvelous deeds among all the peoples.

1 Chronicles 16:23–24

We must always have old memories and young hopes.

—ARSEN HOUSSAY

Open Hands

A Moment to Pause

Consider inviting someone over for tea, for soup and salad, or for an impromptu dinner. It doesn't have to be much. You don't need the right china or crystal, matching linens and napkins, or a gourmet meal. The accessories are long forgotten, but the memory of a relaxing time with friends lingers far beyond the occasion.

Put aside all thoughts of daily pressures or deadlines, or whether your house is clean enough for company. Just wear your best welcoming smile. Remember, you're not simply entertaining; you are inviting someone in so she can feel valued and cared for, where relationships can be developed and nurtured. Your kitchen can be the place to iron out the world's wrinkles, a cozy room for small talk, or a safe haven for someone who needs to share a deep and secret hurt.

And should your doorbell ring sometime when the house is a mess or you're not quite put together, answer it anyway. Unwelcome visitors sometimes bring unexpected blessings.

The beauty of the house is order; the blessing of the house is contentment. The glory of the house is hospitality. The crown of the house is godliness.
—Fireplace Proverb

A Moment to Reflect

Caring enough to open your hand in hospitality opens your heart as well. And as you take time to extend yourself in your busy life, you will find the delight in hospitality. You'll feel more caring, more gracious, more warm and rested.

When you invite others in even for a quick cup of coffee and a packaged muffin, you are modeling God's heart, his concern, and his kindness. And when you get weary and need refreshment, he is waiting to welcome you in the same way: with warmth and love and total attention.

Hospitality is a test for godliness because those who are selfish do not like strangers (especially needy ones) to intrude upon their private lives. They prefer their own friends who share their lifestyle. Only the humble have the necessary resources to give of themselves to those who could never give of themselves in return.

—Erwin Lutzer

Be joyful in hope, patient in affliction, faithful in prayer.

Romans 12:12

A Moment to Refresh

Let mutual love continue. Do not neglect to show hospitality to strangers, for by doing that some have entertained angels without knowing it.

Hebrews 13:1–2 NRSV

If anyone speaks, he should do it as one speaking the very words of God. If anyone serves, he should do it with the strength God provides, so that in all things God may be praised through Jesus Christ. To him be the glory and the power for ever and ever.

1 Peter 4:11

Dear friend, you are faithful in what you are doing for the brothers, even though they are strangers to you. They have told the church about your love. You will do well to send them on their way in a manner worthy of God.

3 John 5–6

If the world seems cold to you, kindle fires to warm it.

—Author Unknown

Share with God's people who are in need. Practice hospitality.

Romans 12:13

We ought therefore to show hospitality to such men so that we may work together for the truth.

3 John 8

Every day they continued to meet together in the temple courts. They broke bread in their homes and ate together with glad and sincere hearts, praising God and enjoying the favor of all the people. And the Lord added to their number daily those who were being saved.

Acts 2:46–47

We proclaim to you what we have seen and heard, so that you also may have fellowship with us. And our fellowship is with the Father and with his Son, Jesus Christ.

1 John 1:3

Who practices hospitality entertains God himself.

—Author Unknown

Other books in the Soul Retreats™ series:

Soul Retreats™ for Busy People
Soul Retreats™ for Moms
Soul Retreats™ for Teachers

All available from your favorite bookstore.
We would like to hear from you.
Please send your comments about this book to:

Inspirio™, *the gift group of Zondervan*
Attn: Product Development
Grand Rapids, Michigan 49530
www.inspirio.com

Our mission:
To produce distinctively Christian gifts that point people to God's Word
with refreshing messages and innovative designs.

inspirio™